ADVANCED BATON TRAINING

FOR
EXPANDABLE AND FIXED BATONS
THE ALBRECHT METHOD

Police Bujitsu Club, LLC

FOR LAW ENFORCEMENT AGENCIES Everywhere

Written By
GARY G. ALBRECHT

The author has made every effort to ensure the accuracy of the information contained in this book. The author and publisher of this book disclaim any liability, including liability for negligence, for any personal injury, property damage, or any other loss, damage, cost, claim, or expense including claims for consequential damages that the reader or others may suffer from following any of the methods of instruction provided in this book. The reader of this book recognizes and accepts this disclaimer of Liability by the author and publisher and the reader assumes the risks of using the techniques displayed in this book.

ADVANCED BATON TRAINING

FOR
EXPANDABLE AND FIXED BATONS
THE ALBRECHT METHOD

Police Bujitsu Club, LLC

FOR LAW ENFORCEMENT AGENCIES Everywhere

Written By
GARY G. ALBRECHT

Harrison House Publishing

Advanced Baton Training
All Rights Reserved
Copyright © 2015 Gary G. Albrecht
v2.0

PUBLISHER'S NOTE

The opinions expressed in this manuscript are solely the opinions of the author in addition, do not represent the opinions or thoughts of the Publisher. The author has represented and warranted full ownership and/or legal right to publish all the materials in this book.

The publisher does not have any control over and does not assume any responsibility for author or third party websites or their content.

This book may not be reproduced, transmitted, or stored in whole or in part by any means, including graphic, electronic, or mechanical without the express written consent of the publisher except in the case of brief quotations embodied in critical articles and reviews. Any reproductions without written permission from the publisher is illegal and punishable by law. Please purchase only from authorized distributors to protect the author's rights.

Harrison House Publishing
www.theharrisonhousepublishing.com
info@theharrisonhousepublising.com
ISBN: 978-0-9861071-2-2
Library of Congress Control Number: 2015952722
Harrison House Publishing and the "HH" logo are trademarks belonging to Harrison House Publishing.
PRINTED IN THE UNITED STATES OF AMERICA

Table of Contents

Advanced Baton

Acknowledgement	1—2
Foreword	3—6
Introduction	7—8
Self Defense Dynamics	9

CHAPTER 1
Martial Arts Principles, Baton Dynamics — 11

Line of Danger	12
Push-Pull Principle	13
Inner Voice	14—16
Ten Cycle Breathing and Control	17
Dynamics of Expandable and Fixed Batons	18—19
Drawing Baton	20—21
Quick Snap	21—22
Thumb Up Draw	23—25
Clearing	26—27
Drawing & Quick Extension Fixed Baton	28
Blocks and Drills	29—34

CHAPTER 2
Baton & Uniform Grabs — 35

Baton Grabs	36—38
Forward Row	39—40
Forward Row Throw	40—41
Inside or Back Row	42—43
Inside Back Row	44—45
Push-Pull Release with Takedown	46—49
Uniform Grab 1	50—51
Uniform Grab 2	51—53

CHAPTER 3
GRABS ON OFFICERS   54

Wrist Grab Single Hand... 55—56
Wrist Grab From Strike .... 57—59
Dangerous Wrist Grab (*Turning the Arm Over*) .... 60—61
Bear Hug .... 62—65

CHAPTER 4
ANATOMY, STRIKES, & COME-A-LONG   66

Shoulder Anatomy .... 67—68
Weakest Anatomical Position 68
Arm Anatomy for (*Crushing the Devil*)....................................... 69
Crushing the Devil .... 70—73
Shoulder Lock (*Short End of Baton*) 74
Entangle the Arm (*Wax-On*) .... 75—76
Side Block Hip Takedown .... 77—78
Single Arm Come-A-Long .... 79—83
Gary's Strike and Takedown (*Fixed Baton*) .... 84—87
Gary's Strike and Takedown (*Expandable Baton*) .... 88—92)

BONUS MOVE
Vehicle Extraction with Baton   93

Vehicle Extraction with Takedown .... 94—102
Standing Prisoner .... 103—105

CLOSING   106

THANKS TO ALL POLICE OFFICERS
AND POLICE AGENCIES

ACKNOWLEDGMENTS

It was a great pleasure doing this book and the presentation to go with it. Without the help of the following persons, this book would have been a real chore. I can not express enough, the appreciation I have for the people that have helped me write this book.

ANDRIES CANE

It is hard to start at a point where my thanks could even scratch the surface for all Andy has done for me. Not only the help and guidance he has given to me on this book, but the many years as my sensei, and a close personal friend. The help with this book comes with the encouragement that he gave me to write it. Thank you Andy for all the help through the past 25 plus years. You have always given me direction in my life as well as in the martial arts world. Thanks........

Officer Reynaldo Bustos

My many thanks to Rey who did a lot of work as my "Uke" to get the right pictures for this book. He also was in a video that was shot for the introduction in the course. He is a wonderful and patient man, an outstanding officer, and a person I am proud to call my friend. Thank you for everything Rey.

Officer Jose Andrade

I would like to give a special thanks to Jose for assisting me as the suspect in the vehicle extractions, that I preformed all these techniques on. He has assisted me now in two books, and has done a great job. He is always willing to assist when he can. Thanks Jose, you have done a great job, and I am looking forward to years of martial arts with you as a student as well as an instructor.

Joseph Rodriguez

With my lack of computer skills, it has kept Joseph very busy. Joseph has helped so much, day and night, as Tech support not only on the book but on the power point presentation for this course. Without his help, I don't know where I would be. He also did a wonderful job as a photographer for this book. My special thanks to a great friend, and a real pal.

Raul Marin

This is another close friend, and he has assisted me in teaching my classes for the Police Bujitsu Club. Raul was also a student of Andries Cane for many years, and the artist for our logo. The part he played was not in the book itself but in the presentation portion of this course, and as the driver of the vehicle, he put on a good show. Raul has been a great friend for more that 30 years.

Vera Mendoza

I also want to thank my wonderful wife for supporting me and giving me the time it took away from us to do this book. Thanks to her guidance, encouragement, endless editing skills, and the use of her artistic eye in helping design the book cover and photo arrangements, it helped make this book possible. She is also in the video portion of the presentation. All my Love to her.

Michael Mendoza-Brahm

It was a pleasure having our nephew assist in the final pictures to finish this book. Retakes of pictures had to be taken for several important things. A special thanks for his participation and bringing his humor, good sportsmanship, and help to complete this book.

With the help and inspiration from my family and friends, this book and training course has come together. I believe it will be a great success. One final thanks. I thank <u>God</u>. I thank him for these wonderful people in my life, and the life he has given me.

FOREWARD

As a young boy I was always fascinated by feats of strength and our many super heroes of the time. I was never too fond of school work and was what I would call an average student. I guess you could call me more of a doer than a thinker. Not knowing what I may be good at, I tried many sports from grade school on. I was small boned and short in stature but was blessed in being an above average athlete. I first tried track and field and became a very good sprinter and competitive in the other field events.

While in junior high school I excelled in physical fitness completing record times in sprints, rope climbing, pushups, situps, and anything physical I could find. It was here in junior high school that I found a teacher that was very special in my life, Mr. Ben Heron. He was a science teacher who also taught a special class of trampoline and tumbling early in the morning before school started. I took one look at this and knew that I wanted to learn this skill. He welcomed me and taught me many things. After a few months, I was doing exhibitions of tumbling and trampoline work at half time of basketball games and at other events. I developed a great sense of balance and kinesthetic awareness from tumbling which was a solid basis for excelling in other sports. After a year of tumbling and trampoline training, I was lucky enough to meet the second teacher who had a lasting effect on my life, Mr. Beuler who was the coach of the swimming and diving team. He had seen me do tumbling and trampoline work and asked me to dive for the swim team at the State meet. I told him I did not know how to dive but he said he had seen me tumble and I would be able to learn diving and why not give it a try? After being instructed that afternoon on the fine points of diving I was told the State meet was in two days, so I would have two days to learn how to dive. To my great surprise, I finished second in my first diving competition at state level. After swimming and diving for a few months I thought I found my sport. I became a speed swimmer and broke multiple records in the 50 and 100 meter events in several different strokes.

When I got to high school, I found that physical educations was all but eliminated, so I tried out for the track and football teams and was good enough to set school and state records, I enjoyed sports but realized that was not going to be able to make a career of sports so in my last two years of high school, I worked nights in a hospital and went to school during the day thinking this might be the path I needed to follow in life.

After high school, I went to Dickinson State University in North Dakota where I enrolled in their nursing program. I had received multiple scholarship offers to

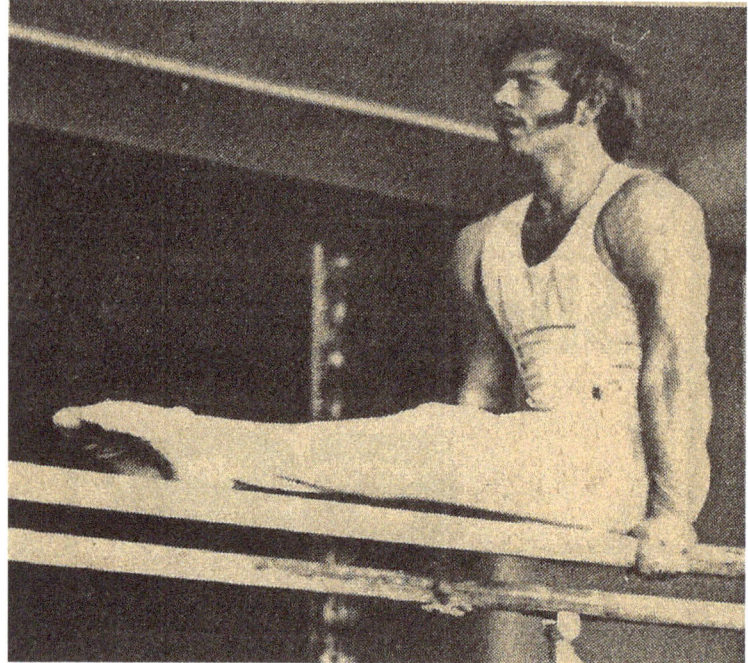

play college football but at only 150 pounds, I decided that might not be the path for me to follow but soon after my arrival in college that urge to compete was back. There was a great gymnastic program at the university and my new roommate had been a gymnast for several years. Again I thought "Why not give it a try?". As a walk on without a scholarship, I made the team and became a gymnast and competed throughout the country and competed in international competitions. Gymnastics developed an even better physical awareness and balance in my life.

I graduated from college and worked only a short time as a nurse in a hospital in North Dakota before the urge to do something more physical as my life's work hit me and I knew I had to go. I joined the U.S. Air Force and volunteered for the

elite Para Rescue Service. Para Rescue in the Air Force is the equivalent of the other services Special Forces (Army Delta Force, Navy Seal Teams) so needless to say this filled my need for something physical and I was also able to use my medical training to boot! I thought I had found my niche for life, but as fate would have it, this was not to be. I was injured in a diving accident which eliminated me from the Air Force. After I left the Air force, I was still looking for that physical training that I had been looking for since childhood. I found two things that peaked my interests, body building and martial arts.

I took a dare from a friend to compete in a body building contest and I found that I could compete and I made a go of it for a couple of years competing all over the country and won multiple amateur titles. In my last competition, I won Southwest Mr. America.

After several years of moving from state to state while competing in bodybuilding, I had the opportunity to study different styles of martial arts under several different sensei's. While never having the opportunity to really follow up and continue with one specific form, after settling in San Antonio, I was fortunate enough to meet Mr. Andries Cane. I became his student in the American Budo-kan style. Mr. Cane had been a worldwide competitor in Judo and through years of study in Europe and Japan had studied Judo, Jujitsu, Bujitsu, and Aikido. He had received eleven black belts in these various martial arts. While studying under Mr. Cane, I joined the San Antonio Police Department and quickly realized these martial art skills could be incorporated into police training tactics.

    During my development in martial skills, I studied the formal and informal styles. I took special interest in the informal training which was incorporated into training police officers. I had become an instructor with Mr. Cane and after many years working with him, he retired and gave me the honor of taking over the forty years of his lifelong work. I have developed the Police Bujitsu Club where his work is still honored, practiced and has been developed into training for police agencies all over the United States through hands on training and by the publishing of these training books.

YOU CAN MAKE A DIFFERENCE

INTRODUCTION

Out of all weapons in history, a stick is probably the most available "Field Expedient Weapon" that a person has access to as a combat weapon. Uses range from riot control, prisoner control, and as a secondary close quarter combat weapon. As in police work, the expandable baton and fixed baton are the sticks that are used in almost every agency. Using them as a secondary weapon for the protection and survival of the officer, will help to keep the "use of force" continuum from escalating to deadly force unless necessary.

In law enforcement, even the smallest departments attend an academy for training. Agencies vary in the training and qualifications offered to their officers. Training also differs from state to state, and from laws to tactics.

No matter where you are, the well trained officer is both effective and safe knowing that it is a standard practice for agencies to have periodic qualifications with their handguns. Why should it be less important to have intermediate weapons training which is used much more in an officer's career? Like firearms training, new weapons, new courses, updates, and new practices are always being inserted into the training of the officers.

Until now, there were no resources available for most departments to run an in-house type of training program; a program that would upgrade the training of their officers and give them more life saving training for the officers on the street.

This course is for agencies that require their officers to carry an expandable baton or a fixed baton, as well as the other many collapsible batons on the market. Special workshops for the training of your officers, as well as workshops to train certified instructors are offered through this course. Information can be obtained by contacting.

Gary G. Albrecht
Phone: 210-215-4787
pbctraining08@yahoo.com

Police Bujitsu Club, LLC
By
Gary G. Albrecht

This is not just a book. It is actually a four hour course designed to have you develop a better understanding and working knowledge of the expandable baton and fixed baton techniques. It will allow you to go beyond the simple basics that you were taught at the beginning of your law enforcement career. As a course, it will show you how the <u>Expandable Baton</u> and <u>Fixed Baton</u> go from a simple impact weapon, which is what officers have been taught for many years, to a high-end tactical weapon, and as a book, it will give you something you will be able to go back to for a reference on the techniques that are being used. It will show blocks and strikes, strategically placed, so as to allow follow-up moves, takedowns, and submissions to immobilize an attacker. This course will also allow you to develop muscle memory in the simple blocking and striking drills. These drills will allow you to become more familiar with your expandable baton or fixed baton and make you confident in their use. I hope to give you more tools in this baton course than in any other baton course offered anywhere.

Using the expandable batons and batons in the manner that is described in this course always should be used as part of the, "use of force" continuum, protecting you as well as your agency from <u>'use of force' lawsuits.</u>
<u>All rights reserved. No unauthorized reproduction allowed</u> .

Gary G. Albrecht
© Copyright 2008
Second Edition 2015

SELF DEFENSE DYNAMICS
OF
THE EXPANDABLE BATON

The batons that fit this description are called many different things by as many companies that have made them. Let's start with the many names for the type of baton that is compact and upon touch of a button or the swing of the baton expands into a full length baton. Of course the full length varies which will be addressed next. The names given to this type of baton of which we will start with is EXPANDABLE; TELESCOPING; TACTICAL; COIL; AUTOMATIC; COLLAPSIBLE; SPRING COSH; BALL BEARING ACTION; AND SPRING LOADED to name several that are on the market today. These names do not change the basic action of this baton. The thing that makes the batons differ in it's effectiveness in real life is, **" Is it an effective and a reliable intermediate weapon?"** In choosing this type of a baton as an intermediate weapon there must be some questions that need to be answered.

1. Will this baton be effective in a real life situation?
2. Will this baton perform as it is suppose to?
3. Will this baton be durable or last through an attack, without breaking down or bending?
4. Is the training with this baton reasonable or just put together to make it look effective?

The answering of these few questions may be helpful in your decision to choose the correct baton for you or your department.

Before answering these questions, let's look at two more factors that some departments have made a variable in their decisions to choose one of these batons. The choice of finishes and the length of the baton. Like the number of companies and many names for the same type of baton, there are almost as many finishes and lengths. The finishes are BLACK; CHROME; SILVER; GUNMETAL; STEEL; URETHANE; ALUMINUM; NICKLE; and PLASTIC. There also may be others out there that may be missing.

Now last but not least in the big decision of choice, the length of the baton. The lengths also have a wide range starting from small to large beginning at 8"; 10"; 12"; 14"; 16"; 18"; 20"; 21"; 22"; 24"; 26"; 28"; 29": 30" and 31". There are even some half inch sizes in between depending on the company that makes it.

The final deciding factor of which usually makes or breaks the deal for departments when having to purchase for an entire department is the price of which the decided baton can be purchased.

The prices vary as much as the sizes, ranging from $21.94 to $165.00 and everywhere in between. But if this is the only factor that is taken into consideration, remember as in most cases, things of any value, you get what you pay for.

Something that is not of a major importance but a necessity is the holster for your baton. These also have different material ways. They come in leather, nylon, and plastic. Like holsters for your weapon, but not with so many safeties, some are just open, some have snap locks, some are covered, and a few other locking devises so they do not fall out.

I have tried and worked with many of these batons on the market before I even wrote the first training manual and had come to a conclusion which I considered the best out there. But before I tell you which one I have chosen, I will tell you some of the shortcomings of the batons on the market.

During my trials with these batons I looked for durability and strength. What I mean is ones that do not bend when they are used. I found several on the market that after a few good hits did bend, and in fact they were worthless after the first few strikes. As for the strength part, it was not just if it could hold up under use, but was it able to make an impact on what was hit, whether a bone at a joint or soft tissue such as a side or a thigh. I did find several that did **not** leave the impact that should be desired in an impact weapon. This simply told the subject being struck, that this weapon does not have the capacity to take control of him or her and the combat would continue. ***"IT DIDN'T HURT"*** You have to take into consideration this person you are having your encounter with, has that same amount of adrenalin in his or her body as you do at this time. If used as an impact weapon, the strike has to breed control. Which brings us to another of our questions. Can the baton perform the function it is intended to do? As an expandable baton, the length is a major factor, not only in strikes, but can it perform as a tactical tool for takedowns and locks? More power is gained in a longer baton, as well as more leverage.

You will find in this course that the use of your baton as an ***impact*** weapon is not a proponent. Let's come from the "cave man" times from beating a person or animal to the 21first century. Learning what the baton can do other than be used as a club, may make the use of your baton a completely different tool in your arsenal of weaponry. You see - joint locks, come longs, and takedowns make your baton a better secondary weapon as well as give you multiple uses.

CHAPTER

1

Martial Arts Principles
Baton Dynamics

I am going to start this book with a few things that need to have a little understanding, before we venture into the baton and the tactics. These few items will make you more aware and may give you the edge that you may need to come out victorious in case of an attack or confrontation that you will have to handle. These four things will make you react faster and may give you an alertness that you have never had before. I feel these are four of the items should be brought to light to give you a little better understanding why the techniques that will be taught are taught in this way. I think this will give you a tactical advantage not with just a weapon but to give you a mental edge.

The four are Line Of Danger, The Push– Pull Principle, The Inner Voice, and The Ten Cycle Method of Breathing Control. These items may all help you, not only in this course, but throughout your life.

LINE OF DANGER

We are going to start with a part of the alertness that is hard to learn. The reason it is so hard to learn is because you have to overcome simple reflex action. Think of someone taking a swing or punch at you. Most automatic responses is to back away from or block the incoming punch, which is a normal response. Let's look at the punch or swing with a different perspective. Where do you think the most dangerous part of this punch will be? Breaking it down—the punch or swing when the person first clenches his fist at that second—has no or very little power. Of course, your reflexes would have to be very fast to stop it at this point. Now the punch or swing is coming, it does not generate its maximum power and speed until the end of the swing, **RIGHT**? This is the most dangerous point of the punch. What happens if the punch is stopped in the middle half way? Now the punch is a lot more ineffective. So the *line of danger* is where the most damage can occur, at the end of a punch. This also works with a kick, the swing of a stick or club. Now, with this in mind when the swing is interrupted prior to striking you, you have to agree that there is less power, and less potential to causing you injury if struck in the middle of the swing. Take a look at a boxer in a ring fight, when he finds himself in trouble or partially injured, where does he go? Does he step back to get pummeled with more punches? **OR** Does he get inside and clench to protect himself where the punches don't have half the damage as if he would standing out and away from the guy beating the heck out of him? Simple principal to understand but not quite as easy to apply this when something comes down.

It does take practice, and a new way of thinking, to overcome what we may have been doing for all of our lives.

PUSH-PULL PRINCIPLE

This technique is another that you have to think and overcome your previous habits from your past. Looking back on your past, think how many times that someone has or attempted to take something from you by grabbing it and yanking or pulling it out of your hands. Now, think of your response. Let me guess when this person grabbed the item and pulled, you pulled back even harder, then it was a matter of who pulled the hardest got it. **<u>RIGHT?</u>** So who ever was bigger and stronger usually won the tug of war.

Lets take a brief look at the art of AIKIDO. In this art, the object is not to exert your power and strength over your opponent but to allow you to redirect his energy to work against him. Any time that power from a punch or the power from a pull is directed toward you, you have the ability to turn this into a redirection. The power that your attacker or opponent applies, can all be increased against him or her by adding your power behind theirs. You might think that this seems to be a difficult thing to do. Taking into consideration that the person you are fighting is twice your size and may even be two or three times as strong as you. Seeing an Aikido demonstration, a small women or man throwing a large attacker around like he was a little kid appears to be impossible, but happens to be a realistic event. Well, it is really a simple principle, and comes with some practice to get very good. Fighting a person that is good in Aikido is like fighting an empty jacket—there is no resistance. I know that like most people you want it *now*. Ok, let's go with a lesser time to train and practice. The object is not to make you an Aikido player, but to understand this principle.

When a force is applied against something, whether pulled, hit, or pushed, it still has momentum, power, and energy. This can all be redirected if the power is allowed to go in the direction of its intent. Look at our first scenario where someone pulls something from your hands. If at the time of his pull, you do not resist with your pull back against it, but you this time push. The power of his pull is now increased by your push, which is easily redirected. Hence, when an attacker or an opponent pulls you, you respond with a push, and when the attacker or opponent pushes you, you respond with a pull. The Push-Pull principle works very well, it is a matter of you being aware and having a response to the action whether it is the push or pull. This response will knock your attacker or opponent off balance as well as give you an opportunity to redirect his energy in a direction that will allow you to be at the advantage by using a technique control and subdue your attacker.

The Inner Voice

This portion of the book is something that needs to be addressed, but yet it is hard to explain exactly what it is. What I mean is that most people have experienced it in their life, or at least have heard of it. Yes, that <u>*little voice*</u>, that <u>*inner voice,*</u> that <u>*special feeling,*</u> that <u>*precognition,*</u> that tells us something is wrong, watch out, be careful. Whatever it tells you and wherever it comes from, it is something that we need to listen to. Whether you call it a guardian angel, an instinct, or the voice of God himself, this is something that we should learn to listen to. That special voice or whatever you want to call it is there for a purpose, <u>**YOUR SAFETY**</u>.

I know that you have heard stories of persons that had that inner voice say not to get on the airplane, and listened to it. Then shortly after, the plane crashed, or something bad happened.

I have heard stories of many officers in the field, having that same feeling, or that little voice telling them something is wrong, or dangerous. The ones that listened are alive to tell about it. I don't believe it is just luck but that there is something to it that is put out there for our protection.

I am sure this has happened many times in my life, and I thought, "***Wow***, it was lucky I didn't do that."

I am going to tell you the first time, as a police officer, when this phenomena really came to my attention and may have saved my life.

Well, it was late at night in San Antonio, Texas, about 2:30 am or so, the night was warm and I am a rookie officer, working dog watch. I had been on the police department only a year or so, when I observed a motorcycle break some traffic law. I don't recall the traffic offense that the rider broke to get my attention at this time, but I am going to make the stop. I do remember the rider, because he was flying his colors. The sleeveless dirty blue jean jacket with the "BANDIDOS" on the back, and what was suppose to be a white t-shirt under it. I remember him wearing dirty blue jeans, and black boots, and a helmet. The helmet was a state law at that time, but it was black and skinned up with deep gouges and scrapes on it. The motorcycle of course was a Harley, black in color, and a lot of chrome on the engine as well as other parts, such as the long kick stand and the mirrors on each side of the handle bars.

I lit up my patrol car's lights using the emergency lights, which squeaked and made a slight groaning sound as they turned around and around. The rider was on the inside lane when I had hit my lights, and he pulled to the right across the outside lane to the side of the road where the curb was.

Making the stop, with all this in mind—being a motorcycle gang member, he was a big guy at that, night time, not many people around, and not asking for cover—I was a little uneasy, lets put it this way, a little nervous too. I told myself, "Well this feeling is just because I am a rookie, and it's natural to feel this way."

As the biker comes to a stop on the side of the road, I see his feet come down, and can see him looking side to side. He then reaches back with his left foot, kicking down the long kick stand. He never looks back at me, but tries to see what I am doing by watching through his mirrors, by moving the handlebars back and forth to get a good view.

This is the time that "little voice" from within me says, "There is something wrong, it's just not right, and do not approach the bike like you usually do." I open my door, and leave it open, then went back around to the rear of my patrol car, and approached from the right side , while watching the biker. I take my time and watch around as I approached. I could see the biker was watching his left mirror moving the front fork back and forth. The sound of the bike still running helped my approach from being heard. I got almost next to the biker when I asked him for his drivers license and insurance. The biker jumped as I spoke, not expecting me on that side of the bike. I could see that he was nervous, but what the heck, so was I. I asked him to turn off his bike and step over to the sidewalk. I could see he was uncomfortable, and he hesitated, then looked around a few times before complying. With a good police tactical stance, I observed him closely as he pulls out a large black folding wallet on the end of a chain, and gives me his drivers license. I checked him on the information channel since we did not have computers in our cars at that time. The biker came back with warrants, so I placed him in handcuffs right away. When searching him, I found some cocaine in his inside jacket pocket as well. We did not have protective cages in our patrol cars at this time, so I sat him down at the curb while I called for the wrecker. The wrecker just took a short time getting there, and I barely had time to get all his information down on my paper work.

When it came time for the wrecker to put the straps on the bike and take it to the pound, I saw that the left handle bar was different than the right. The left handle bar was about six inches longer and was made with a hinge toward the end of it. I looked carefully at the mirror on the left side, and I saw cross hairs marked into the mirror like on a rifle scope. I was able to open the hinge and found a loaded shot gun shell, chambered in the handle bar. This was for all purposes a shot gun that aims back behind the rider through the end of the handle bar. After the biker was placed in my patrol car, and we were on the way downtown, the biker stated he was going to kill me as I approached him on the left side when I got close. But, I screwed the entire thing up by approaching on the other side.

I would like to give you one more example of that inner voice that had happened to one of the officers.

Officer L. was new on the force, but he was a born warrior who chose Law Enforcement as his career. It didn't take him long to build a reputation for efficiency and dependability, even before he faced his greatest challenge.

It happened one evening just before dark when a speeding car rocketed past him; radar showed the vehicle well over the posted limit.

With his emergency lights on, siren wailing, he was soon close behind the speeder. The vehicle slowed and pulled over to the curb, and officer L. stopped about 20 feet behind the speeder.

He opened his patrol car door, and stepped out picking up his hat and citation book. Officer L. began walking toward the driver's side until he was almost to the back bumper when suddenly, without knowing why, he jumped sideways behind the car. As he did so, the driver twisted his body, swung his right arm out of the window and fired two rounds where officer L. should have been.

Officer L. pulled his weapon, firing through the back window, killing the gunman.

From that moment on, he told every officer to pay attention and respond to their feelings, and listen to that voice—— INSIDE.

I am sure you have also heard of many incidences that have happened to officers, family, or even yourself.

LISTEN AND TRUST THESE INNER FEELINGS OR VOICES

IT'S YOUR LIFE THAT'S AT STAKE, COME HOME SAFE AND ALIVE TO YOUR FAMILY.

THE TEN CYCLE METHOD OF BREATHING AND CONTROL

This is a short but true story to explain "The Ten Cycle Method of Breathing and Control". Written by my sensei, Andries Cane.

"In my late teen years, I was competing in judo and doing very well; however, occasionally I would lose a match to a competitor I knew I should have beaten. I asked my sensei to tell me what caused me to lose. **"You got mad and lost control."** Was his terse reply. I asked, " Well, how do I keep from getting mad?" He smiled (he knew he had me) and answered, " You don't know how to breath." He smiled again and walked away. I hurried after him, and got his attention and pursued it further. "What do you mean, I don't know how to breath? How am I supposed to breath?" He pointed toward my navel and answered, "Breath down there and breath slowly. That way you'll always have control."

I followed his advice and for the next three years won the U.S. Army Black Belt Championships."

I found that by controlling your breath, you control yourself. The ABK system of breath control is called the TEN CYCLE METHOD which has now been passed down by me, Gary Albrecht for the Police Bujitsu Club. One cycle consists of one complete inhale and one complete exhale. Control your rate of breath to ten or less per minute and you will always maintain emotional control. Practice every day in everything you do until it becomes an automatic body response and you no longer have to consciously direct it. Especially notice your rate of breathing when you become stressed, and slow it down immediately. With practice, your normal breathing rate will stay below 10 respirations per minute.

The initial purpose of control is to enable you to use the powerful self-defense skills you are learning only when it is really unavoidable. In Budo and Bujitsi, you immediately are able to hurt another person, and hurt them badly. You need this to aid yourself against unprovoked attacks, but remember this, every time you embroil yourself in a physical fight, you put yourself in danger. Circumstances can change quickly— the unarmed man now has a knife or gun; the single man you thought to wipe the floor with now has four very large friends who want to tear your limbs from your body. You must decide an appropriate response to aggressive people who want to goad you into a fight, but to do this, you must be in control of yourself. This doesn't mean swallowing your anger, but by using your breathing to keep you from losing your temper and lashing out.

SIMPLE DYNAMICS OF THE EXPANDABLE BATON AND FIXED BATON

HOLDING YOUR BATON

Since the expandable baton and the fixed baton differ somewhat due to size, the grip will vary some also. The expandable baton length is a factor, I suggest due to practicality in my courses to use the 24", 26", 28" 29" and the 31". In martial arts, a weapon in your hand can become an extension of your own body, or without good training, it just eliminates one hand in a altercation. Thus with correct training, the longer baton will give you a longer reach and distance if you should need it, as well as a great tool for take downs, locks, and submissions. The smaller size batons may not allow you the extension needed for take downs and locks.

As fixed batons go, I suggest that a baton should be 24", 26", 28" as much as 32". The standard baton used in police work is 26", and there is a long 36" baton of which is used as a "riot" baton, mainly for a two hand control.

When gripping the expandable baton, there is a need to have about a half of a hand's width sticking out below your grip, or at least 3" from the butt end of the baton. This end protruding below the heel of your hand has multiple functions. The tip extending is the thickest and heaviest end of your baton and can be used as a striking tool if needed to gain a submission or a tactical advantage. The tip is also used in placing a suspect or assailant in a hooking or locking movement to gain control. All of which will allow movement to a submission or the immobilization of your prisoner. " *YES, THE BATON CAN BE USED FOR MORE THAN JUST STRIKING*".

The grip used on a fixed baton is a little different. Most fixed batons have what is known as a grommet on the baton that serves more than one purpose. One of its jobs is to secure the baton from sliding through your baton loop. In some cases, this grommet is rubber, and other cases, it may be built as part of the baton. This grommet is where you hold onto the baton, allowing the baton to pivot at this point and be used as a fulcrum from where the baton is swung from.

Knowing that a stick is probably the oldest weapon known to man, we have moved past the Neanderthal stage in life and hope that we are a little more intelligent. The baton is **_NOT_** just an impact weapon. Now, all we need is a little training to get us out of this mindset, and someone to show you what can be done to accomplish the control that is necessary to subdue someone in a violent attack.

It is understandable that a two handed grip on the baton is a stronger grip, and it will allow a faster response to an attack. It also gives you support when blocking a blow coming at you, where one handed will collapse much easier. It is also understandable that the block will not be as effective if it doesn't make it to its mark in time. Increasing your speed when using two handed blocking takes a little understanding of your muscle control. When gripping a baton with your two hands, allow your grip to be firm but do not grip tight. The tight grip will cause the flexing of more muscles in your arms. The more muscles that are flexed and ridged in your arms will cause a slower response. The response that will be fastest is an involuntary response from the fast twitch muscles. If you have to think about it. If you have to use the mind to tell you, you need to move your arms, the response will be way to slow and even to late. Try it both ways just by bringing your arms up to a front blocking position and you will see and feel the difference.

DRAWING YOUR BATON

Let's first go with the expandable baton. Of course the drawing your baton depends on the way you carry it on your belt. I know that different companies make different types of holsters for the expandable batons. Like holsters for your weapon some are better than others, and like holsters for your weapon, you become good with what you have, if you practice with it. Knowing that you most likely will never use a fast draw on your baton but a smooth transition from your holster to your hand, and the opening of your baton all in one smooth movement will be a little more intimidating. The psychological viewpoint from the attackers perspective, seeing that the baton is drawn and expanded with little or no effort is a show of confidence and this officer may know how to use it. This display may be all is needed to bring him down from his anger or rage, bring him back to the real world.

Taking a quick look at the types of holsters that are on the market, assuming you are going to carry your baton in a holster, I have seen batons carried in the pockets, back pockets, front pockets, and pockets in the leg of your pants. I feel that there are too many variables in doing this, and the baton is not as accessible as you may want it to be. The main problem would be that your pants are made of a soft flexible material for comfort on your skin not to support a baton. The baton may get entangled in the cloth, or something already in your pocket, or fall into the pocket so you have to dig for it. Most departments do require a holster made for your baton and the material that matches your gear on your belt. Materials that baton holsters are made of can vary from leather, nylon, and to the new space age type plastics. They also vary in the way the baton is secured in them. Some have a snap with a leather or nylon strap that comes over the top of the baton. Some just fit down tight in the holster. Usually leather can create a problem in getting it in and out unless you work with it a little and break it in. Also, be aware leather swells in moist conditions. Nylon seems to be pretty consistent in shape and no problem with swelling. The plastic ones are hard and fixed in form. Some have a little problem with the baton being too loose, or the baton not locking in place. I have found that some of the plastic carriers have a locking device to hold the baton in place at the end of the carrier. Sometimes the officer will have to push and turn his baton slightly in place after it is returned to the holster, this may secure it a little better. The holsters also may be fixed in place in the upright position, such as with the leather and nylon holsters, which may make it a problem if you are wanting to carry it in the front. Bending over may cause the holster and baton to dig into your abdomen on the top or bottom, or even both which will only give you the option to carry it on the side or behind you.

Remember your decision to place your holster needs to be one that you will be able to work with so you have easy access to when you need to draw your baton. Some plastic holsters have a swivel so you are able to change the angle from which you carry your baton, that may give you a few more options.

The preferred side, if carrying your baton behind you on your belt is to carry it on your strong hand side. I personally carry mine in front as a cross draw. This seems to be easier to get at when drawing, and easier to defend if someone should ever try to take it from you. You also may take into consideration that reaching behind you requires much more flexibility especially if your holster is a little sticky from rain or other reasons. Lets face it as we get older you do not have the flexibility we did in our twenties.

The draw on expandable baton can be with the thumb down or thumb up position. By saying the thumb down position I mean the end of the baton that extends is at the thumb side of your grip. The thumb down allows you to have a stronger extension of the baton when you swing it open. A directed extension toward an on coming attacker is another option. This expansion of the baton that will be shown and is what is called a "Quick Snap" which extends the baton into the attacker as he approaches.

Quick Snap
Extension of Expandable Baton

Figure (1A) When the baton is drawn, keep the non-baton hand up and open in case of a fast approach or attack, that you may have to fend off before the baton is fully deployed. The baton could be used as a quick extension to the solar plexus, or to deflect a strike as shown in moves to come.

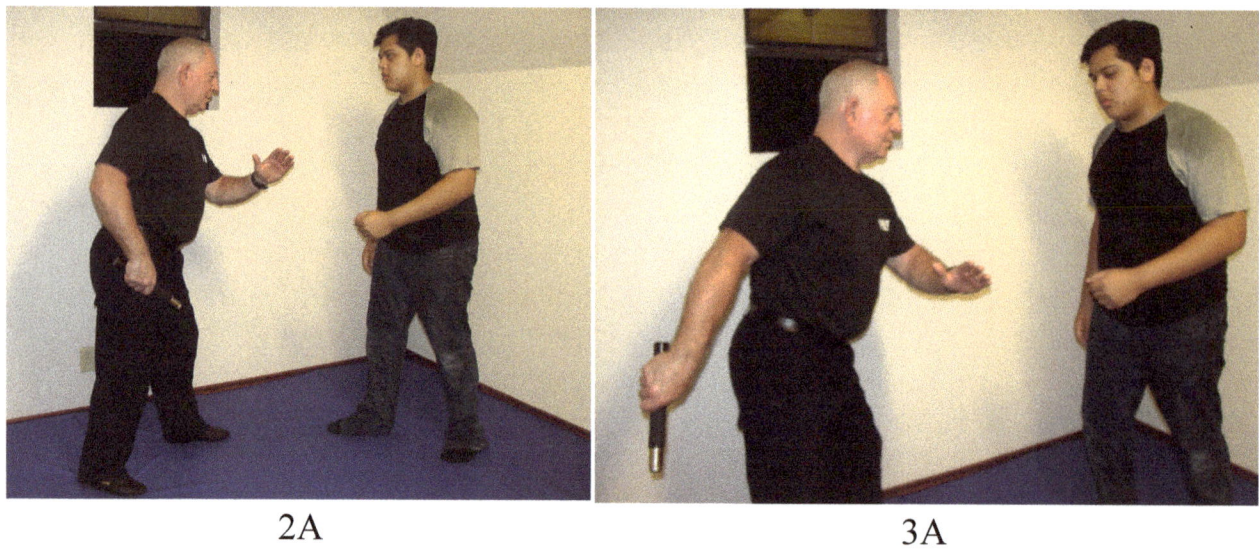

2A 3A

Figures (2A) and (3A) Keeping your body in an up right position slightly leaning forward, and not telegraphing your movement by looking down. The baton is brought back quickly along side your hip and just passed you buttocks to allow a good quick but fast swing for a good snap of the baton.

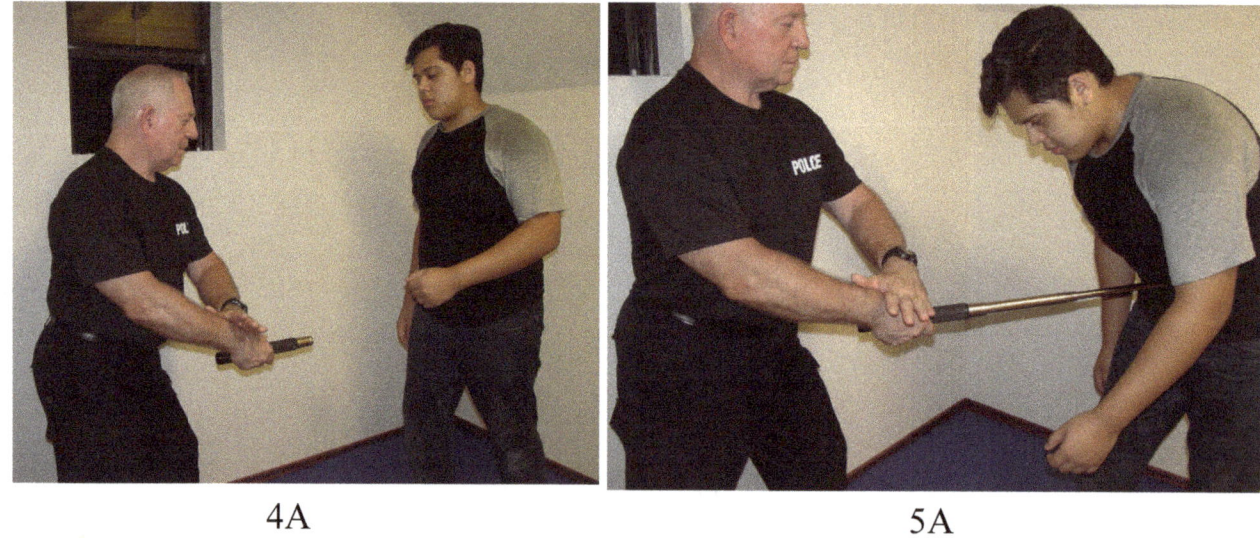

4A 5A

Figure (4A) Your baton is brought forward quickly with a snapping movement at the wrist and your free hand is brought down at the top of your hand above the thumb just below the wrist to make a sudden stop of the baton hand as it is coming forward.

Figure (5A) The sudden stop of the baton hand in the fast forward motion as well as the snapping motion will extend the baton hard and fast. The targets you should try for are the lower extremities, such as the abdomen and the genital area. Keep the baton hand pointed forward not upward or downward. With very little practice, you will be able to be fairly accurate with the tip of your baton.

Thumb Up
Draw and Extension of Expandable Baton

The thumb up allows you to draw the baton and keep it hidden behind the arm in a ready position until it is expanded. This also allows the baton to be used to strike pressure point.

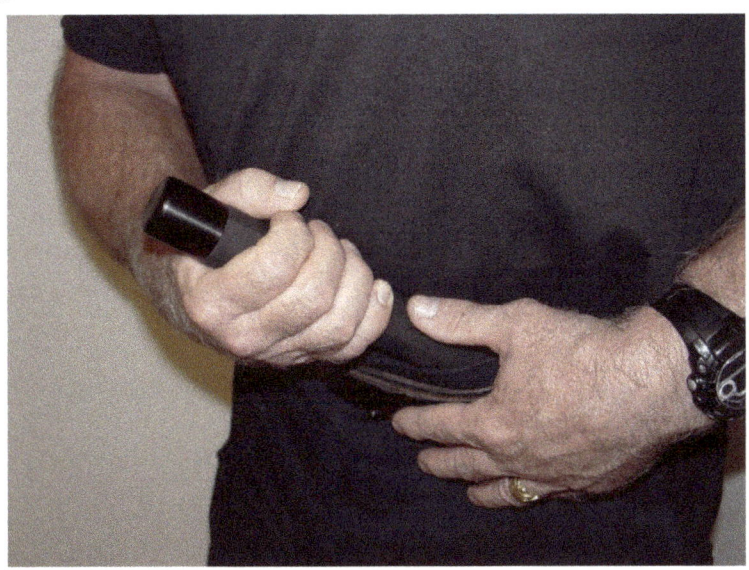

6A

Figure (6A) The draw in this picture is from the belt and not from the baton holster where it is usually carried, as well as showing a cross draw, which some officers use.

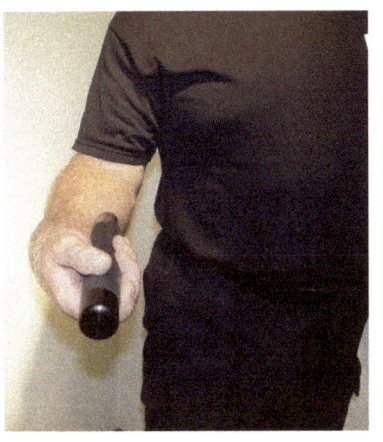
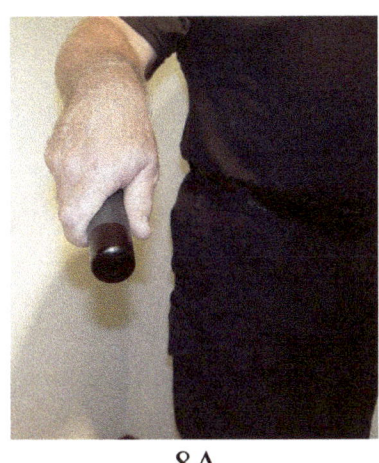
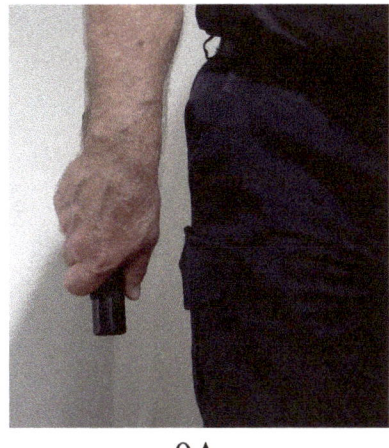

7A   8A   9A

Figures (7A), (8A), and (9A) These three picture show easy concealment with the closed expandable baton which also works when the baton is expanded.

10A

Figure (10A) This is a close quarter draw that does extend the short end into the attacker's solar plexus.

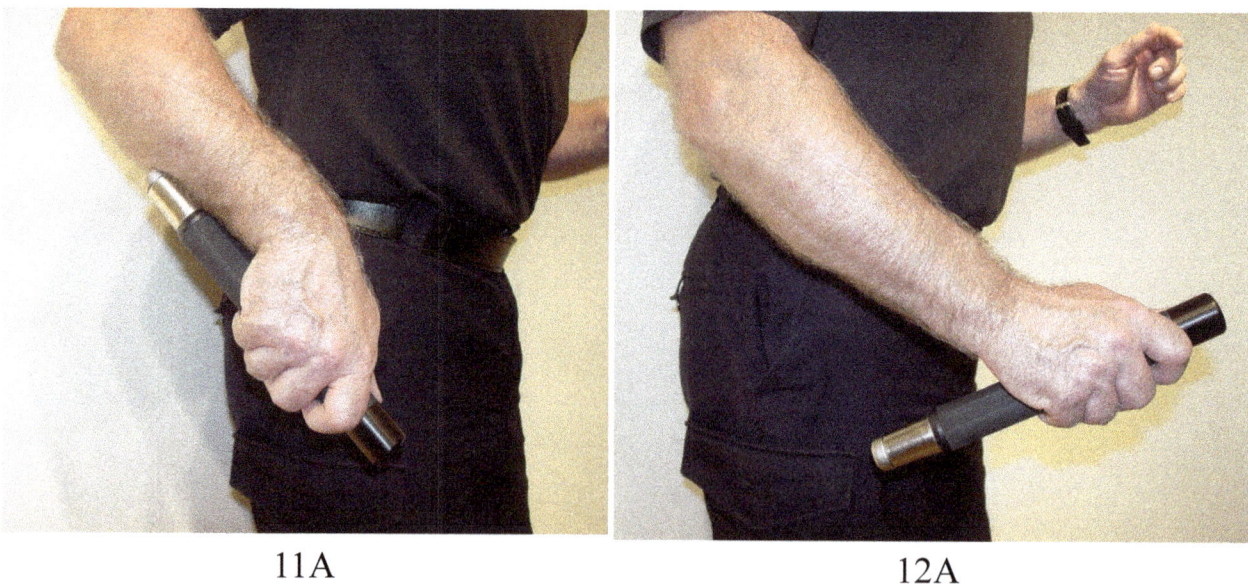

11A   12A

Figure (11A) The expansion of the baton in the thumbs up position is done by dropping the baton down by the hip with the thumb pointing down on the baton and cock the end of the baton back to the wrist.

Figure (12A) Start your swing to extend your baton by bringing your wrist forward and upward cocking your wrist back at the same time as you bring your arm forward in front of you.

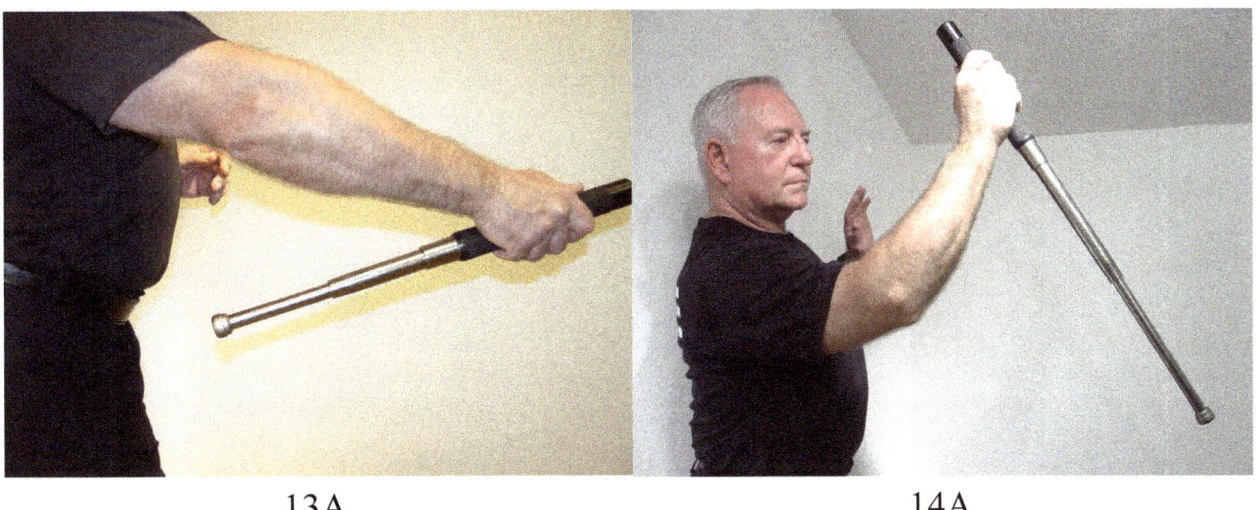

13A 14A

Figure (13A) and (14A) Completing the forward swing in a circular motion upward flexing your wrist back at the end of the motion snapping the baton to its fully expanded position.

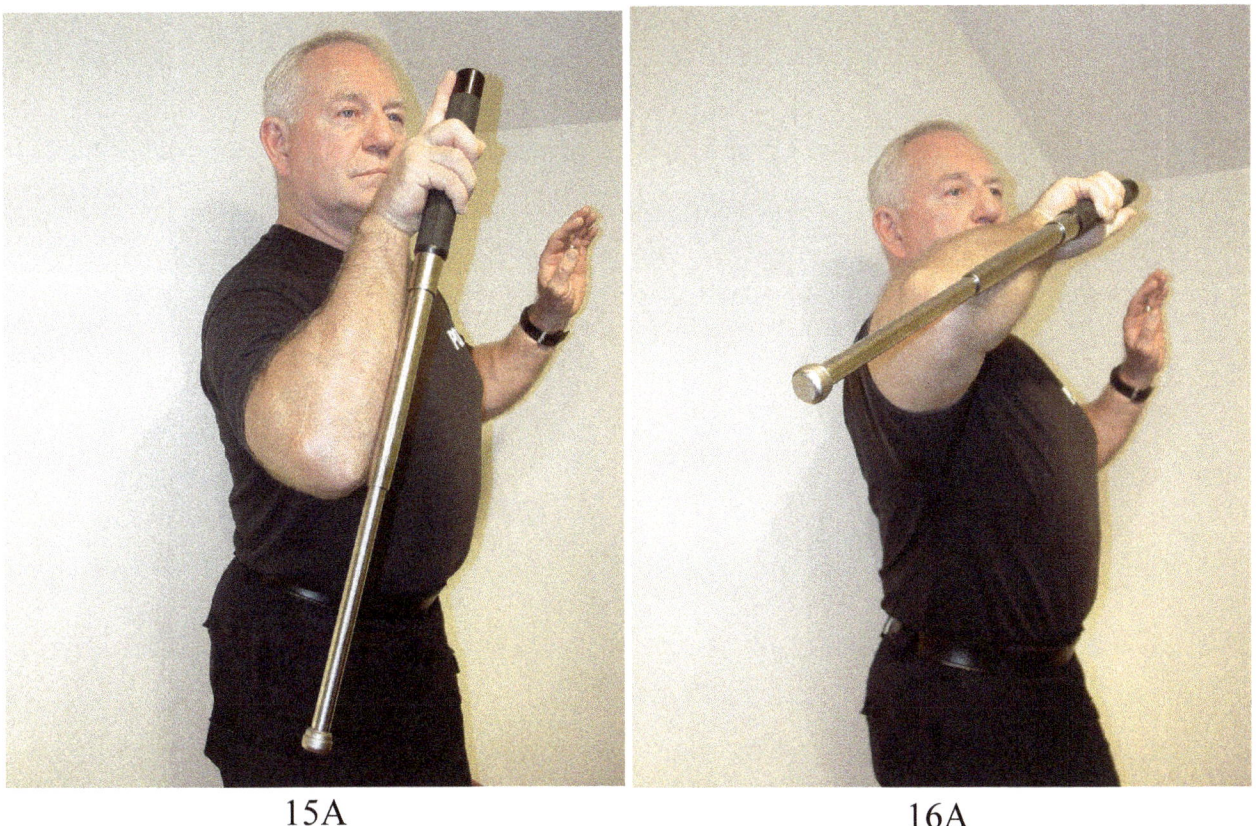

15A 16A

Figure (15A) Bring your baton down to your forearm with your forearm vertical as this will allow you a defensive stance used to stop a side blow.

Figure (16A) Turning your forearm more in a horizontal position with the baton pulled tightly to the forearm will allow you to defend against an overhead blow.

CLEARING

This is when a situation may de-escalate, but you still want the person to move the person to a side to allow you to pass or get by, and not strike them. It is more of a push than anything. Just a movement to **_Clear_** a path for you to get by.

Figure (17A) With the baton at your forearm in a forearm defensive position, bring your non support hand to the short end of the baton in a forward gripping position, thumb down.

Figure (18A) Step to your strong side as you grip with your supporting hand.

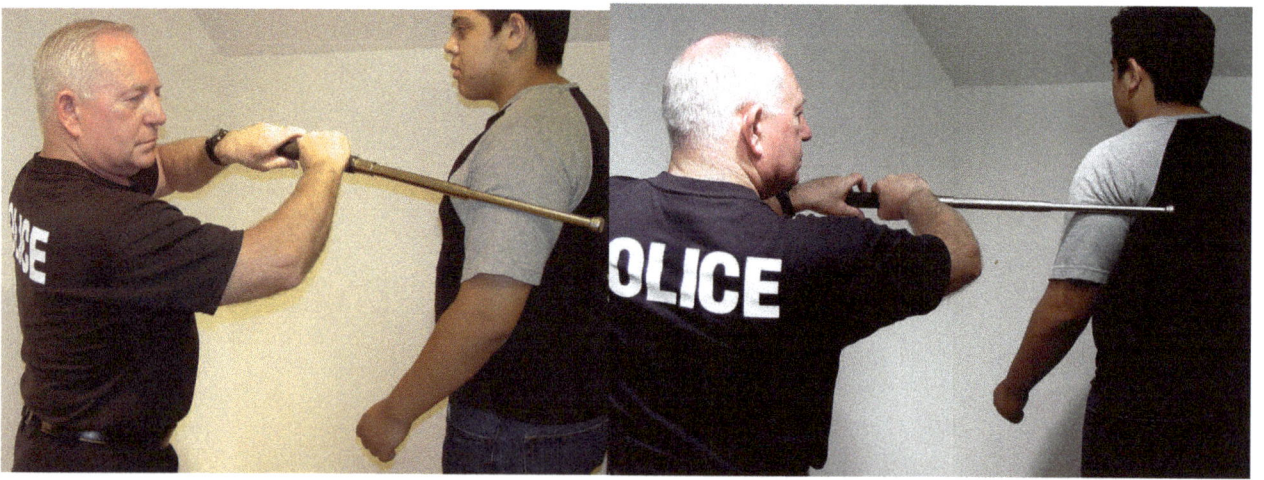

Figure (19A) Place the baton on the upper arm of the person that you intend to move by pushing your strong hand forward. Make it obvious that you are not striking, but trying to get him to move so you can get by.

Figure (20A) Push your baton so it slides around the arm, so that you are turning his body away from you so you are no longer facing him. This is at a moderate speed, so it does not appear that you are striking him, but just pushing him to the side to clear the way so you or another officer may pass.

21A

Figure (21A) As you extend your baton around his arm and to the back of his arm, the end of the baton will be on his back. While this is all going on, your inside leg steps back and around to maintain your balance and square your body so it is not twisted. This will allow you to apply pressure to the baton. Putting your subject in this position gives you a little advantage in distance, if he should try to turn back toward you to fight. Most of the pressure is placed on strong hand in a pushing movement with you arm being extended. Your support hand is pulling back on the short end of the baton keeping the pressure on the front tip of the baton.

Drawing
Of A Fixed Baton

The fixed baton does not have the holster problems, but also does not collapse or is not able to be carried on the belt as compacted as the expandable baton. There are metal rings and plastic rings to carry it on your belt. There is a small problem that it has to be taken off the belt when getting in and out of your vehicle. This also means that you have to remember to reach for it in your vehicle each time you get out of your vehicle. Some people consider it a problem having a long baton swinging along side of their leg, and even having it get entangled in their legs or bouncing back and forth if they have to run. The upside to the fixed baton is a visible intimidation factor. It is carried either on one side or the other due to the length. When drawing the baton, it also can be drawn with your thumb in the up or down position. The draw is a long draw due to the length of the baton where a little more space is required. The fixed baton can be carried on either side. When drawing this baton on your strong side, it has to be right behind your weapon which causes a little inconvenience in getting at it when drawn, as well as being close to your weapon if it should be needed. Then there is the cross draw which is the other alternative when carrying it on your weak side. This sometimes takes two hands to draw it, due to being on the opposite side. Your weak hand will tilt the baton forward as you take your grip with your strong hand across in front of you.

The Quick Extension of the fixed baton is a close quarter draw that extends the short end of your baton into an oncoming attacker into his ribs or abdomen.

Quick Extension
Of Fixed Baton

3A

Figure (3A) This picture shows the draw of the baton on the strong side. As the attacker comes at you, your grip on the baton is a thumbs up grip. When the attacker Approaches, the baton is thrust forward into his abdomen. Notice that the left hand is brought up to protect against any attack to your face or head.

BLOCKS AND DRILLS

Blocking strikes and kicks is a skill in itself. If the blocking comes from the martial arts world, it can take quite some time to learn feet positioning. But in the real world of police work, we can not spend a long period of time on just this one thing. The learning has to be quick and efficient. To make this as simple and effective as possible, blocking attacks from the front has to cover the entire body from head to toe and left to right. Now with this in mind, we can divide the body into four easy to remember quadrants.

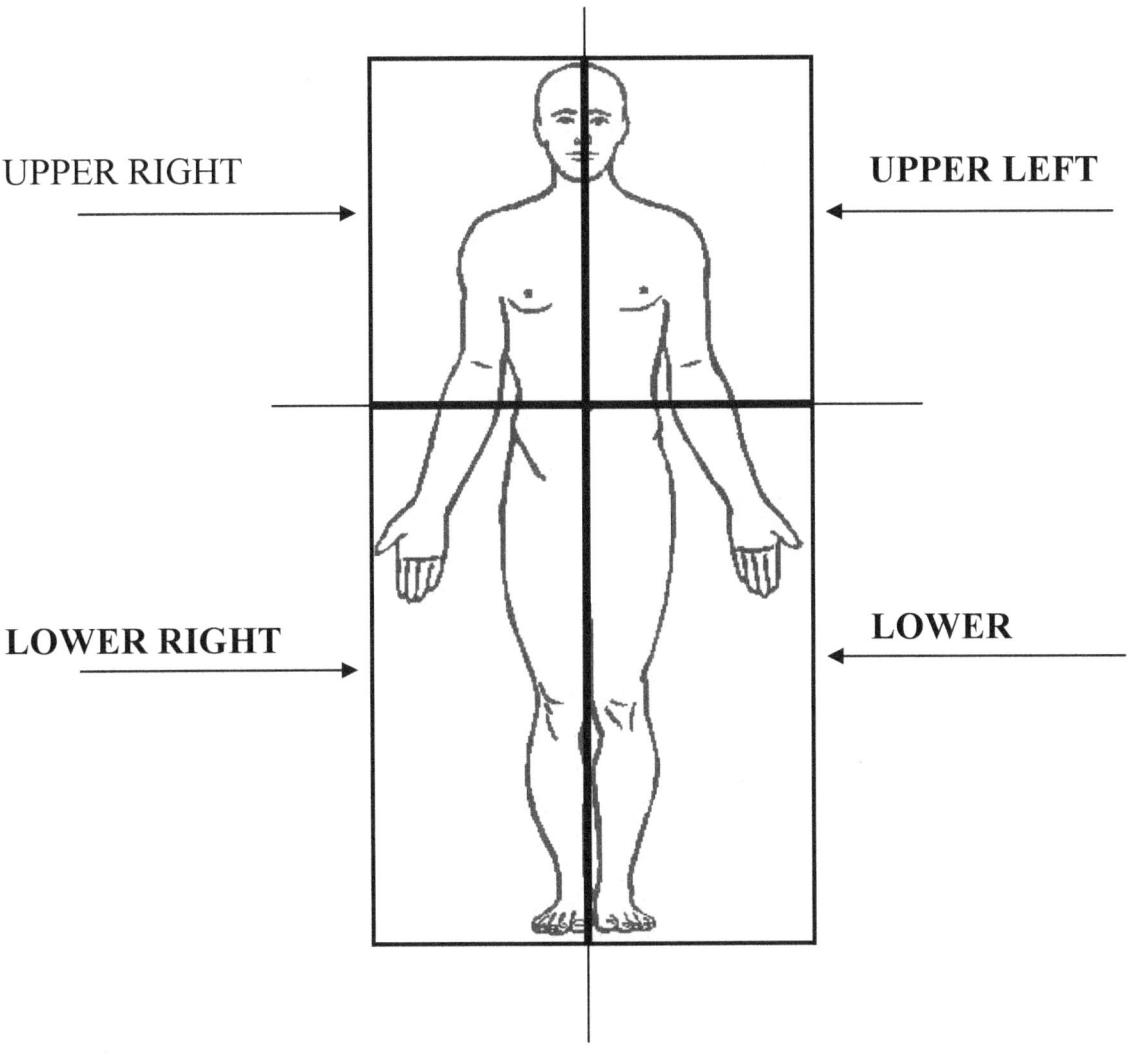

Now think how you would have to protect the front of your body in the easiest movement. Imagine yourself holding your baton in both hands across the midline of your body. By bringing your arms up in front of you to a position over the top of your head, you have now blocked the upper right and upper left quadrants of your body from a frontal attack. Well, it is not quite that easy remember that I said the block must be simple but effective. The simple part is bringing the arms up in front of you to catch the attack with an effective block. The block has to be strong enough to withstand the blow and fast enough to make it to the oncoming blow to prevent it from making contact with your body. The two-handed grip is very important on your baton, and will give you enough support to block a blow as long as your grip is at both ends of the baton. A one-handed block against a hard strike will not be sufficient enough to deflect a hard blow from coming in and possibly causing you injury. Your own baton may even fly back and strike you. Part of the "effective part" of a block comes from the baton being secure in both hands, but there is another part. The baton has to be fast enough to catch the blow. Speed is accomplished with a little practice and knowing that being relaxed and alert to what is going on around you will heighten your awareness. Lets break these two things down to get a better understanding what this means to you.

Alertness, I know seems pretty much a given to most people but there are many things that may come into play. Your stance should be non-aggressive and your baton in a down position. This alertness should be an inner alertness and not be evident in your stance or your expression. Your elbows should be close to your sides, with your feet about 18" wide or shoulder width apart. Allow your senses to heighten— hearing, seeing, smelling, and feeling. Go into our 10 cycle breathing as I had mentioned earlier in this chapter.

The relaxing portion is mint to allow your body to **_not_** be rigid or tight. When the body is rigid, tight, or in a flexed position your reflex time slows down. The faster your reflexes are the faster your response time is.

Reflexes are a nerve signal induced muscular reaction caused by an external stimuli. For example, if a punch or an object is thrown toward your head, your brain will send a signal to your hands to respond to block it before it makes contact. Some people are born with fast reflexes, and others have to practice to attain a quicker reaction time.

Being police officers, most find themselves sitting behind the wheel of your patrol car for hours in the day. You may not be exercising or eating correctly as well. What does all this have to do with reflexes? Do a few things to increase those reflexes and get your mind working at a higher frequency. If you are a runner, run on a trail with varied terrain with uneven footing and small objects. With a slow run, your mind will pick up on the objects on the path causing the mind to alter your average response time. With new terrain and the faster you run, the quicker your reflexes will become. A simpler exercise would be to use a rubber six sided ball, called a reaction ball. It bounces in all different directions when thrown against a wall. If you are not quite so active but choose to do hand eye coordination. There is a good kids game called JACKS that will also help.

Working to improve your peripheral vision will increase your reaction time. The ability to see things coming at you earlier increases that time significantly. Here are a couple of little exercises that will help increase that peripheral vision. First, all you have to do is look out a window that has a good view and focus your vision on a distant object. Keep looking at that object while you slowly let yourself become more aware of objects that surround it on either side. Do this exercise once a day, widening your vision more each time. This exercise will get your brain in the habit of observing more objects in your peripheral vision.

A second exercise would be while walking or riding in your car, make a point to notice peoples hair color, or make of cars as they pop into your peripheral vision.

Well for those who are the video game players you now have an excuse to play a little more. This does increase hand eye coordination, causing you to move from thought to action without pause. The first person shooter and roll player type games often require the most coordination.

Now let's get into the nutrition that can change your reflex action. Foods high in refined sugar and trans fats can make you sluggish. Make sure you are getting enough protein, complex carbohydrates, and healthy fats.

Whole foods like nuts, fish, berries, greens, and garlic
Increases cognitive function
Drink plenty of water, since dehydration can
Lead to lethargy and decrease reflex time.

Certain nutritional supplements have been associated with improved reflexes, cognitive function, and reaction time.

Ginseng, Gingko, Vitamin B-12, Vitamin C
And Omega 3's

Last but not least the subject of getting plenty of sleep. According to the National Institute of Health, sleep helps you have quicker reflexes and perform on a higher level. Both body and brain slow down when you are sleepy, resulting in impairment of your reflex actions. The reflexes are noted to be faster after seven to eight hours sleep.

Doing the following blocks and drills will assist in your response time and allow you to start developing your muscle memory.

BLOCKS AND DRILLS

1B

(1B) Block in a High Position

Bring the baton up from a non aggressive position at your center position, allowing your arms and chest area to be **_relaxed_** to get a faster reaction in a snapping motion to meet the over head blow. Step foreword slightly to meet the attack. If your arms are flexed and ridged, the flexed muscle will be slower to respond in a reflex action.

(2B) Block in a low Position

From the center position keep your back straight, not allowing yourself to bend at the waist, preventing your face or head from being struck by a fist. Step into a kick or lower attack slightly allowing the lead leg to bend so you are able to get down toward the kick or lower attack to protect your groin area from being struck.

2B

Blocking Drill in High and Low Position

Start in a low ready two-handed position. Slowly have your partner swing an overhead blow, as you block with a small step forward and an upward snapping motion to meet the attack. Speed up as you become accustom to the attack. Then have your partner use a stabbing motion to the abdomen or a kick to the groin, again as you make the small step forward bring your baton down to meet the attack. Combine the over head attack, kick, and abdomen stab increasing the speed.

3B

(3B) Block to the Right

Starting from the center position with both hands on your baton. As the attack from the right comes, the baton is brought up with the left hand on top as you step forward with the left foot to allow your body to be more square with the attack to block the oncoming blow. If the right leg should come forward on this attack, you would be twisting you back further than it should be.

4B

(4B) Block to the Left

Starting from the center position with both hands on your baton. Blocking to the left is a mirror image of the block to the right. As the attack comes from the left, the right hand is on top and the step is taken with the right foot as the baton is pushed forward to meet the attack. The step is important to alleviate any stress on the lower back, and giving you a stronger block at contact.

Blocking Drill to the Right and Left

Starting with a right hand attack. While in the low ready position with two hands on the baton, have your partner swing slowly at first with a back hand motion as you step with your left leg slightly forward and your left hand on top as you turn your baton to meet that attack. With the left hand, attack your partner's swings with a forearm strike, as you step with your right leg forward slightly and your right hand will be on the top side of the baton. Practice right and left attacks increasing the speed as you develop muscle memory. When you block, remember to try to take the oncoming attack to the center of the baton to avoid having your fingers struck, and to develop eye-hand coordination with your baton.

Combine High and Low Strikes, Stabs, and Left and Right Attacks

Now combine all attacks 'High, Low, Left, and Right and a Stabbing" motion starting out slow and increase the speed as you progress in skill. Don't get sloppy. **_THINK_** of the attack as it comes. Bring your arms down to center in between the attacks allowing them to be relaxed to increase the speed of your block.

When your partner starts alternating strikes, this will stimulate your responses to catch up and think on a faster level. Have your partner start alternating his strikes at a **_SIX_** count. Six attacks alternating the type of attacks as the attacker sees fit. Switch partners to a person larger or smaller than you, if you are able, to get a different perspective on the size difference. This will allow you to learn there are distance difference due to height as well length of your attacker's arms and legs.

Add Punches, Side Kicks

This small addition to your partners attacks may add just a little quicker response from you that you did not know you had. When he adds this type of attack, it becomes more realistic. Acting like the crazies out on the street, punching and striking at the same time, trying to make contact to injure you. Again slow it down a little to learn how your body responds, before your partner steps it up a notch. The blocking will come natural after you have done this drill several times. Now here comes the part that is the hardest part of Blocking—The ability to read your attacker. **_Slow it down a little again and observe your partner as he has to change his stance and body posture, as he changes his type of attack._** Watching his feet and the way he turns his body. This ability to read the attacker will telegraph to you how you will respond.

Add a Body Check or Jam

This portion of the drill adds again one more facet to all the types of attacks that are being thrown at you. This is when you may have blocked his attacks and now his only alternative is to rush you and just try to take you down or knock you off your feet. Here is where your stances come into play. Having good balance and footing will help guide his attack to one side or the other. You make the decision even if his attack is straight on. Step to the side you choose and make contact with the attacker's shoulder or body if possible to redirect his attack.

CHAPTER 2

BATON & UNIFORM GRABS

GRABS ON THE BATON

When your baton is drawn, there is always a problem with the threat of the baton being grabbed, whether by the attacker or an accomplice of the attacker, to prevent you from using it. With a strong grip from an attacker, it could prevent you from using your baton at all or even have it taken away from you and used against you.

Let's take a look at several different grabs that may occur and what we can do to regain control over your baton.

1C

2C

Figure (1C) When the baton is grabbed from the front a single-handed grip as in figure (1C). Even if the attacker has a very strong grip, there is little control on his part. The object at this point would be just stop you from using your baton. The only thing he can do is to pull or push the baton; twisting would not be probable. With your two handed grip, one on each end of your baton, it would be almost impossible for him to twist it out of your hands.

Figure (2C) To respond to this grab on the baton, you should turn the baton vertically and tilted slightly toward the attacker, so the high end of your baton is over the little finger side and the back of the attackers hand. This should place the attackers hand in a thumb down and little finger up position. This also will put a little bit of a strain on his wrist. This position gives you three large mechanical advantages. First with the arm turned with the thumb down puts stress on the wrist and forearm, causing a good reduction in the grip strength. Second, the wrist has less flexibility moving back toward his wrist, with a short movement in this direction the wrist will lock. The other is the weakening of his grip in the thumb down position. The thumb and index finger will be all that can hold your baton at this point which allows the baton to break loose with little effort on your part.

Figure (3C) The baton should be pushed forward and down across the back of the actors wrist by the top hand. By pulling the bottom of the baton baton toward you at the same time, this will pull the baton out of his grip with relative ease.

Figure (4C) The double grip will propose more of a problem for you. You do not want to get into a push and pull match with an attacker.

The object is for you to gain control right away, and "balance" is first priority. Even if a technique is attempted and you are off balance, most likely it will not work or turn into a real mess, and could be a costly mistake .

5C   6C

Figure (5C) The first thing is to step in with the leg on the side that you will be pushing the baton down on. This should be your strong side, and it will assure your balance during the performance of the technique. If your attacker is stronger than you, standing toe to toe with him is not a good idea. To overcome this problem, you step in to allow you to use your body to assist in turning the baton. As you step in, the baton is turned vertically and slightly tilted toward the attacker. The arm you now have on top is bent slightly and over the top of his hand. This position will give you a physical advantage. Now, you will be able to push down with your upper arm and your shoulder. This move should be done at a quick speed, to avoid the attacker responding to what you are doing.

Figure (6C) Once you have stepped in and your baton is vertical, push the baton down and back across the little finger side of the attacker's top hand. Push down with your arm and shoulder to give you more power, extending the baton down and through his grip with one smooth movement. At the same time you are pushing down, you are also pulling your lower hand back toward your waist. You will find that his top hand will break free first and usually crosses over the top of his bottom hand. You will also find that this push, pull action will pull him forward and off balance.

Practice this movement until it is smooth with a partner. Use caution, especially pushing the baton down across the wrist. If done quickly, your partner may not get his hand to release as quickly as it should. It may cause injury to his wrist. Remember that your partner is there for you to learn with, not to injure.

Forward Rowing
To Break A Double Grab On Baton

When the baton is grabbed from an attacker from the front, the object is to take it away or prevent you from using the baton on him. This technique is used to split his energy and power. Understanding that his focus is to take the baton away with both of his hands. By using this rowing method, his focus is split between his two hands which cuts his strength and energy in half. This now gives you that small window of opportunity to start a technique to break his grip on your baton.

7C

8C

Figure (7C) When the grab occurs, it usually is a quick grab in order to yank or pull the baton from your hands. This goes back to having a good defensive stance so that you are not caught off guard and lose your baton. The old adage comes to mind here, "***EXPECT THE UNEXPECTED***". Your response needs to be fast and spontaneous. When the baton is pulled, step forward with your strong side to prevent you from losing your balance.

Figure (8C) Allow your arm to bend so that the thrust of your baton over his wrist will be with your arms and body as you turn toward his forearm. This also takes you off his line of strength, causing him to turn back. The motion of your baton is now in front of you where you are the strongest. The end of the baton is forced over the little finger side of his hand and wrist, and downwards. This will twist his wrist at an angle, and the force of the baton pushing down will cause him to release the baton. Make sure that the thrust of the baton is followed through and down toward his center below the belt line. Then pull that hand back as the other end of the baton extends forward as your body turns back.

9C

Figure (9C) The baton is brought over the top of the attacker's wrist in the same manner as the first side. The baton is brought forward and comes over the little finger side of the attacker's wrist as your body turns with the motion of the baton. Once the baton is over the top of the wrist, it is pushed downward toward his center line causing his grip to release. **_(Center line meaning his belly button area.)_**

FORWARD ROW THROW

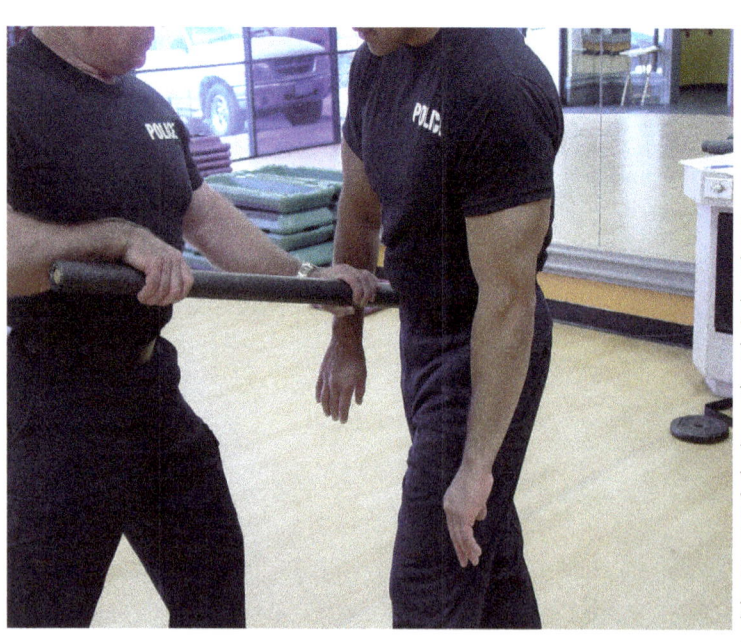
10C

Figure (10C) This can be a continuation of the forward row to escape a two-handed grab on your baton which places your baton in the correct position to throw your attacker to the side. After the grip is broken from your attacker's right hand like in figure (9C), the baton is extended slightly as it is placed under his right arm and along his right side, as you step forward.

40

11C

Figure (11C) The left hand end of the baton hooks under the attacker's right arm as your right hand with the baton is brought forward sharply, striking your attacker in the ribs or mid section. This strike should cause him to bind forward.

12C

Figure (12C) The right hand end of the baton is brought back around his head and placed over the top of his neck. Your left hand is brought up under his right arm as you press down with your right hand. This motion is like turning a large boat wheel. The attacker's balance will be completely off as his left shoulder will drop causing him to fall to his left side as you lift and turn.

INSIDE or BACK ROW
Release From Double Hand Grab

A second release from a two-handed grab of an attacker on your baton comes from the inside. The position is like rowing a boat backwards.

13C

Figure (13C) This starts again with the two-handed grab from your attacker in the attempt to take your baton away. With a good defensive stance, you still need to respond quickly to his first attempt to pull the baton away. As the attacker pulls back, you need to move foreward with his pull, by stepping forward with your strong side. Split his strength by pushing one end of your baton toward the attacker and the other end of your baton to be pulled back toward you. When your attacker feels that one side of the baton is being pulled harder than the other, he will strengthen his grip to that side which will split his strength. His response will be automatic which will weaken his grip on the side that is pushed forward.

14C

Figure (14C) First, step forward to control your balance as you bring the end of the baton under the wrist. Once the baton is hooked under the wrist, it is pulled back and upward toward you as you push your other hand forward.

15C

Figure (15C) When the other end of the baton comes forward, it makes a small loop around the attacker's wrist, hooking that wrist from the inside as you are pulling back and upward. This will break the last grip and place you body at a slight center toward your attacker.

Continuing this *Inside Back Row* as a follow-up to breaking the two-handed grip it can be used as a take down.

Inside Back Row Take Down

16C

Figure (16C) While standing at the centered position, extend your baton across the attacker's body and under the forearm. The end of the baton is allowed to slide slightly in your hand to give you a little extra length to the end that is under his arm. This length will assist in hooking the shoulder as you and the baton turn to that side of the actor's body. **<u>Do Not</u>** allow both of your hands to pass under his arm. As in this picture, observe that the left hand is in front of his wrist. The knuckles are placed on top of his wrist for control over his right hand. With the baton behind his arm, it will prevent him from drawing his arm back. In this position it will allow your left elbow to raise up if his right hand is brought forward in the attempt to hit you.

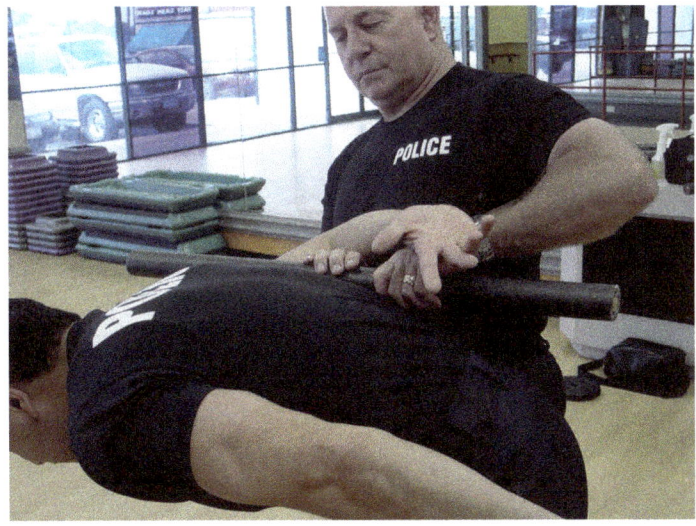
17C

Figure (17C) Leaving your hand under the armpit of the actor as you turn toward him the baton crosses behind his shoulder. Allow your wrist and elbow on the far end of the baton to raise upward to catch the actor's arm as your left arm comes behind him. This will prevent his arm from slipping over the top of yours and allowing him to stand upright. When your left arm turns to his back bending his elbow, it will push the shoulder down causing him to be off balance. Continue

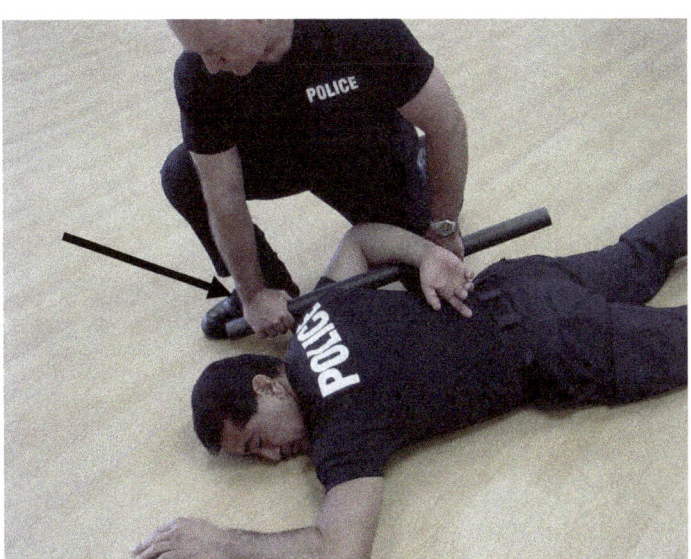
18C

Figure (18C) When the actor becomes prone on the ground change the grip of the first hand that was under his arm to a top position on the baton. This hand will now push down on the baton across the shoulder. The actor's hand will not be able to slip down due to your other hand being vertical holding onto the baton.

PUSH-PULL RELEASE WITH TAKEDOWN

When your baton is grabbed by two hands, the focal point of the actor is on his grip. This will usually be followed by a pull to get the baton away from the officer. This technique does not make the actor release both hands. But when one hand is forced to be released, the tides turn against him allowing the officer to gain an advantage for a good take down.

1D

Figure (1D) The distract is a factor that changes the attacker's focal point. Since his main focus is on his grip of the baton, a short kick to the shin brings his mind to his shin area for a split second. The short snap kick is not to disable him, and does not even have to be painful. The snap kick is done in a fast movement and the foot is brought back to its original position so as not to lose your balance.

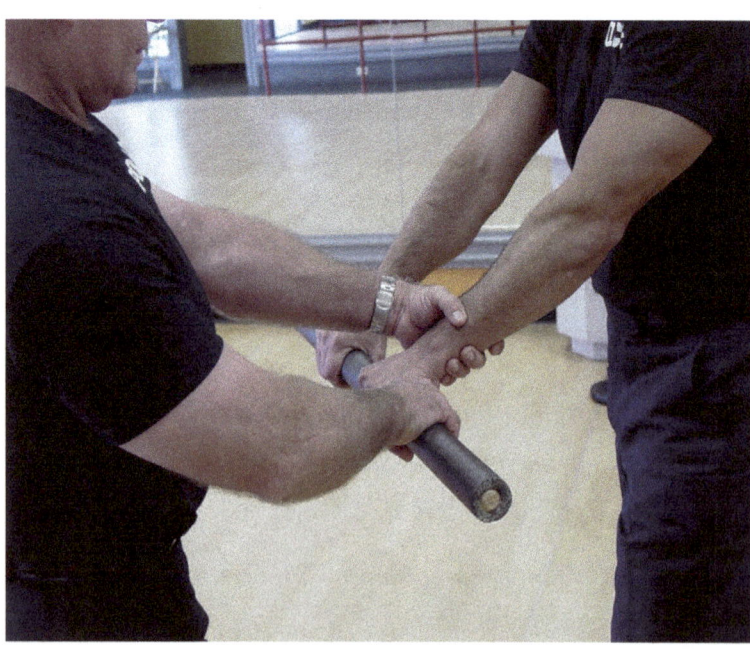

Figure (2D) As soon as the distract with the snap kick is done, release your grip on the baton with your weak hand. Your hand shifts to inside the wrist of the hand, gripping the baton closest to your strong hand. Just before a grip is made on his wrist, reach inside and come back quickly to grip and pull almost in a slapping manner pulling his wrist toward you as you push forward with strong hand. This snapping motion will break his grip on the baton.

3D

Figure (3D) As soon as your grip slaps the inside of the actors wrist, you will be pulling his hand toward you and off the baton. This will also pull him forward and off balance at the same time the push of your baton goes forward with your strong hand. The push should be strong enough to go straight into the actor's ribs stepping forward with the leg on that side. Retain your grip on the actor's wrist with your weak hand pulling him forward, as you are driving the end of the baton into the actor's side.

─────────────────────────DISCUSSION POINT─────────────────────────

To add a little more "striking power" to the strike you deliver to the actor's rib, step forward on the side that your are striking with as you push the end of the baton into his ribs and exhale. After the strike makes contact into the actors ribs, "center circle" back with your left foot to the side you just struck. The "centering circle" I am speaking of is if your right leg is forward your left leg should swing back around you changing the direction that you are standing. This will center you for your balance and have you facing in the same direction as the actor.

4D

Figure (4D) Now that you are behind him maintain your grip on the actor's wrist and extend the far end of the baton in front of the actor at the waistline. Keep the actor's arm extended and facing forward as you place the near end of the baton just above the elbow across the triceps area of his arm.

―――――――――――***DISCUSSION POINT***―――――――――――
"DO NOT CHANGE YOUR GRIP ON THE BATON. KEEP THE UNDER HANDED GRIP. IF YOU ATTEMPT TO CHANGE YOUR GRIP, YOU WOULD HAVE TO LET GO AND TRY TO REGRAB THE BATON. THIS

Figure (5D) Step forward pressing the baton against the back of his arm and keep pressure on his arm by pulling back on the actor's wrist. The pressure across the back of his arm and elbow area is painful and will bend him forward. The step forward with your right foot **_can_** be placed in front of his left leg, but not necessary.

5D

Figure (6D) Continue the forward pressure with the baton, pressing the actor to the ground. Allow yourself to go down on one knee or if need be, both knees. This will prevent you from bending over at the waist and losing balance when his weight shifts from an upright position to the ground.

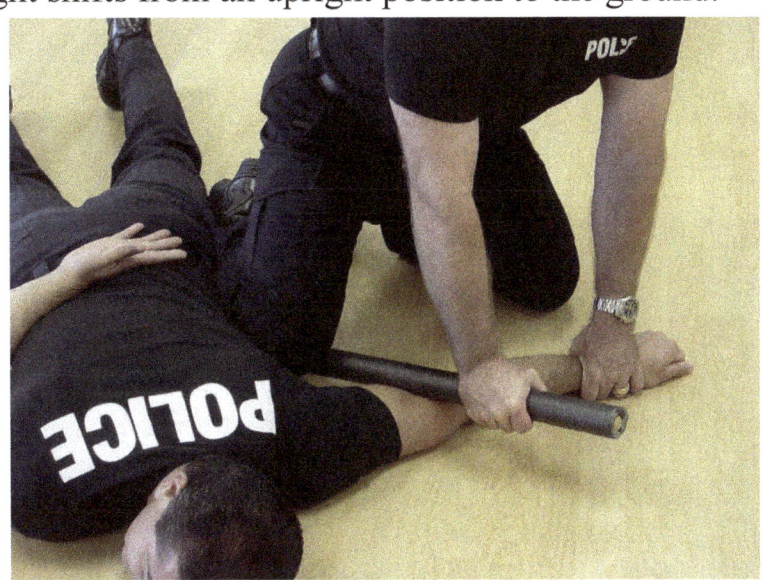

Figure (7D) To make this takedown into a submission position, the inside knee is brought up and placed in the arm pit area of the actor. Your shin will press down on the baton which is painful when the baton is pressed into the back of his triceps. This works as a submismission because it presses down on his shoulder not allowing him to raise up or turn in either direction. This will allow you to direct him to place his hands behind him.

Uniform Grab I
Two Handed Front Uniform Grab

1E

Figure (1E) When an attacker grabs you from the front and your baton is held with both hands in a low ready position. As soon as his hands grabs your uniform or shirt, step back allowing yourself to have a little space between you and the attacker. This also will pull him forward and slightly off balance. This space is needed to allow you to release one hand from the baton and bring it up and across the front of your chest in front of you.

2E

Figure (2E) When your hand comes from under the attacker's arms and meets the bottom of his wrist, the baton is brought down in front of your face and across the back of the attacker's wrists. Your other hand is brought up across your chest at the same time. The baton comes down on top of his wrists and grabbed from the other side. This places the baton across the top of his wrists, and your arms in as "X" position under his arms. Tighten your "X" position as close as you can to prevent him from pulling his hands out.

3E

Figure (3E) Lean forward slightly against his hands, putting pressure back on his fingers. Bring the baton down as you step back and kneel, locking his hands against your chest. Pulling the baton back to your chest as it is across the back of the attacker's wrist.

Uniform Grab II
Two Handed Front Uniform Grab

1F

Figure (1F) This is the same two-handed type of grab from the front to your uniform or shirt. You have your baton in the low ready position with both hands on your baton. As soon as the attacker's hands grab your uniform, step back with one foot allowing your knees to bend slightly. In this case, it is my strong side which is the right foot. This will again pull him forward and slightly off balance.

Figure (2F) The baton is brought forward and up with your weak hand. The baton is placed between the actor's arms and under the his chin. Push the baton forward and the attacker's head back creating a litle distance between you and the attacker.

Figure (3F) As you push the attacker back, release the grip on the weak side of your baton and grab the inside of his wrist as you extend the baton with your strong hand past and to the side of his face as you turn back to the side of the attacker. As the baton extends, you will see the end of it being placed over the arm right below the shoulder and under the arm you are holding. the grip on the attacker's arm is with your thumb up and kee his arm straight and palm forward.

4E

Figure (4F) Turning back to become facing in the same direction as the actor, step back with your left foot pivoting on your right. Keep the arm you have a grip on extended and straight. Step forward with your inside foot, and pushing forward with the end of the baton. The baton will slip off the arm and shoulder of the attacker and move to his midsection. The pressure being placed on the end of the baton across his triceps will cause him to bend over.

5F

Figure (5F) Push the actor to the ground and go to your knees alongside him. If you try to remain standing, you will be bent forward and off balance. The actor's weight will be down on top of the baton and the baton should be at almost a 45% angle from his side and across the back of his arm.

To continue into a submission position, keep the pressure down on the baton across the triceps. This will force his shoulder to the ground and will be very painful across the back of his arm. Bring your knee up to his side over the top of the baton and close to the armpit. Press down with your knee onto the baton. This will allow you to have both hand free if needed.

CHAPTER 3

GRABS ON OFFICERS

GRABS ON OFFICERS
WRIST GRABS

SINGLE HAND CROSS WRIST GRAB

1G

Figure (1G) When the wrist is grabbed in this manner, it is usually to prevent you from using your baton. This is their strong hand to your strong hand. When the grab is on your wrist with the baton in your hand, your hand and baton are not rendered useless or incapacitated in any way. The baton does not have to be switched to your weak hand.

2G

Figure (2G) Release the hand on the baton that is ***not*** being grabbed. With the hand the baton is in, turn it to the inside bringing the baton over the top of the actor's wrist. The free hand will come under the actor's wrist gabbing the baton on the other side as close as possible to the actor's wrist. This will lock the actor's wrist in between.

NOTICE
The grip on your strong hand is not a full grip, so it will allow the baton to come back over the top. The grip is lessened to allow the baton to have enough flexibility to come over the top of the actor's wrist. The grip is now with two or three fingers left on the baton. This will be sufficient to hold the baton through

3G

Figure (3F) After the baton is gripped on the other side of the actors wrist, the actor's wrist is locked. Pull the baton down and forward. He should not be able to release the grip he has on you wrist. The baton is pulled tightly against the back of his wrist pulling him down and forward keeping him off balance by not allowing his trapped hand or arm to touch the ground. Remember that you need to go down to one knee to lower your center so you are not leaning over.

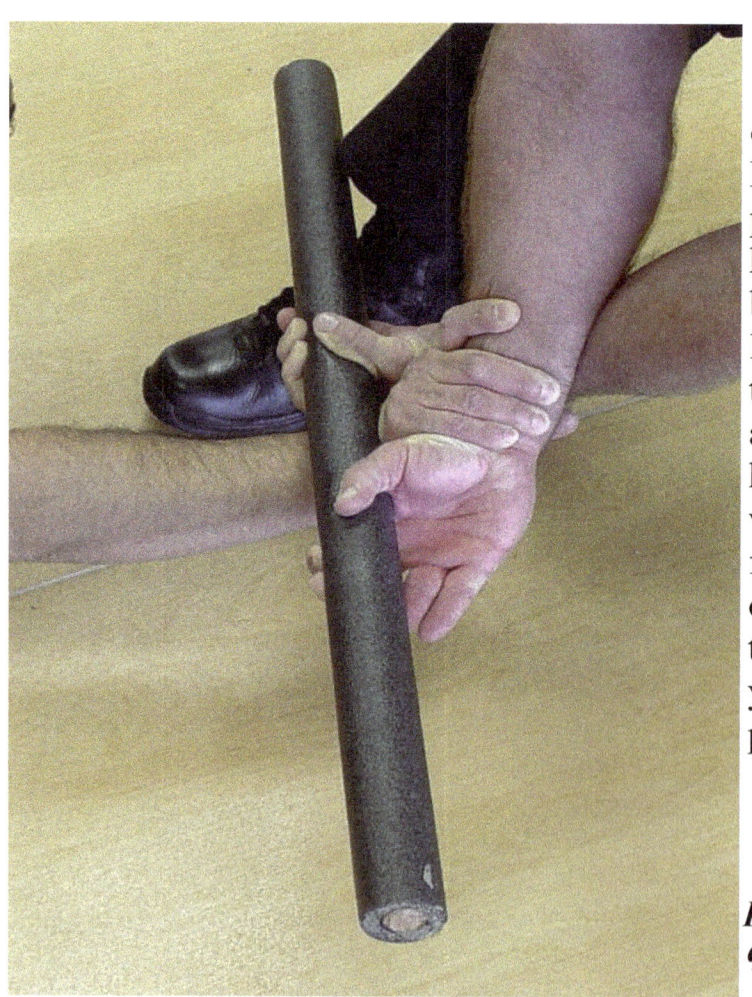

4G

Figure (4F) This is a close up of the grip on the actor's hand. Look at the partial grip explained earlier with the right hand after the baton is turned back across the actor's hand. The left hand has a reverse grip on the baton on the other side of the actor's wrist trapping the actor's hand. By pulling the actor forward extending his arm out in front of him and you being up over the top of the locking position, you will be able to keep your wrist in his hand and pressed back toward him.

CAUTION
When practicing this with a partner do not do this technique quickly. This may cause injury to the wrist.

GRAB ON WRIST FROM STRIKING POSITION

"FEINTING"

1H

2H

Figure (1H) "Feinting" is a pretend blow or attack intended to take the opponent off his guard. In this case it is a set up to give the attacker the opportunity to grab your wrist. Raising your arm and giving him directions to get on the ground or whatever you may want him to do. Place the arm in reach and give him the opportunity to grab your arm for what he thinks will prevent him from getting struck with the baton. When doing this, angle yourself to his near side allowing him to reach up and grab your wrist. Remember that your baton should have several inches protruding beyond the heel of your hand. " NOW YOU GOT HIM JUST WHERE YOU WANT HIM."

Figure (2H) When the grab is made by your actor on your wrist, the end of the baton that extends beyond your grip on the baton is brought over the top of his wrist by rolling your wrist back. When the baton is placed over the top of his wrist, you then reach under his wrist with your free hand in a reverse grip and grab the end of the baton as close as you can along side of the actor's wrist, scissoring it between your wrists. This will lock his wrist and hand as tight as possible between your wrists. Bringing the baton down parallel to your body in front of

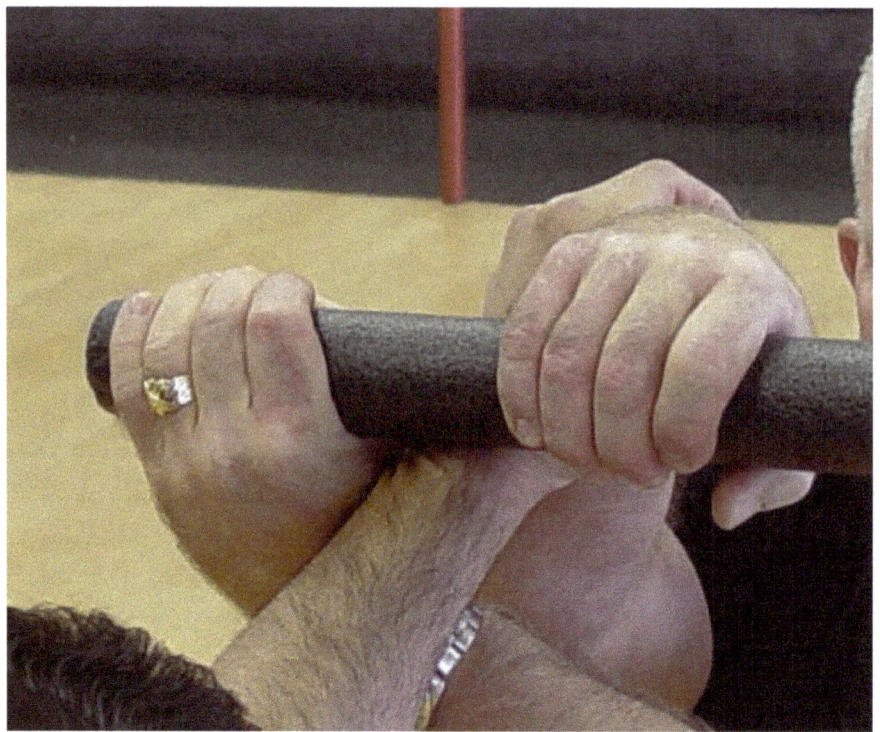
3H

Figure (3H) This is a close up to show you when the baton is brought over the wrist, it is at the base of the actor's wrist. Your free hand is brought under and grips the baton as close as you can to his wrist. Bring the baton down parallel to your chest for the best locking position. It works well, **_BUT_** to give this move a little more power, tilt the baton slightly forward so it is flat across the back of his wrist and as you back up for the takedown it will be a stronger move.

4H

Figure (4H) Once the actor's hand and wrist are trapped, as in figure (3H) tilt the baton flat across the back of his wrist and apply the pressure diagonally across the back of his wrist as you take him down. Back up making him reach forward as you take him to the ground. Remember to kneel down as you take him to the ground so you lower your center and are not bent over once you have him stretched out.

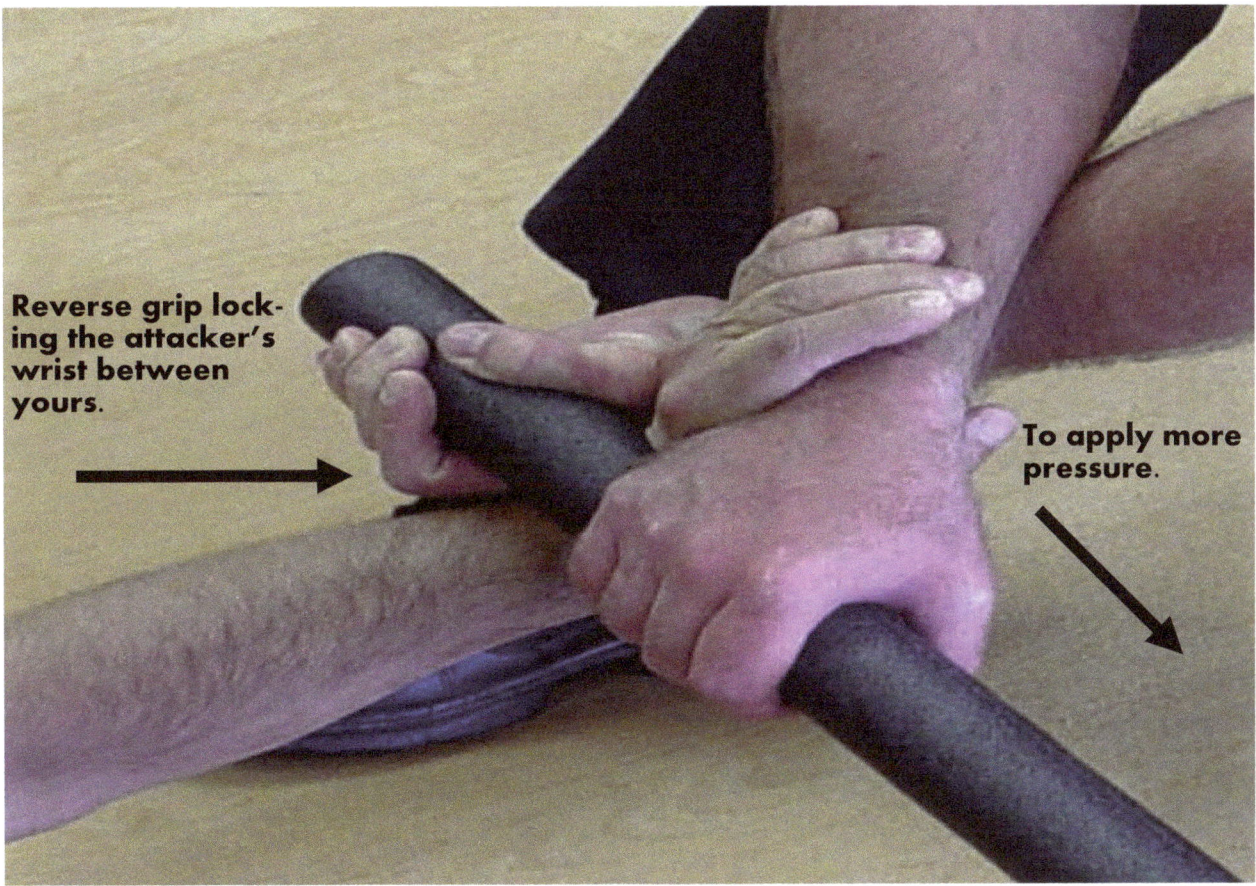

5H

Figure (5H) This close up will give you a better idea how your second hand should grip in a reverse grip and how tight it should be in order to keep his wrist in this lock. A reminder to keep his arm extended out in front of him as you back up and take him down. This squeeze on his wrist, between your wrists, should not allow him to release his grip. The main pressure with the baton is placed on the back of his hand across the index and middle figure.

Once you have your attacker stretched out with his arm extended in front of him, more pressure can now be applied if necessary. Move your baton in the direction of his head diagonally with a little pressure on the baton allowing the long end of the baton to come up a little. This motion forces his wrist to bend back further and places the baton pressure to increase on the carpals and metacarpals of his hand.

"TURNING THE ARM OVER"

Straight Across _Dangerous_ Wrist Grab

Not that any time a person grabs you is not dangerous, but the dangerous wrist grabs have to be responded to quickly or the attacker may injure you or take your weapon. These grabs are not to prevent you from taking action **BUT** to show aggression toward you. **THEY ARE ATTACKING YOU, TO GET AT YOU ANYWAY THEY CAN.** In this case, the grabbing of your wrist is to take control of your arm and your weapon. In this case, the baton that you are carrying could become free and there would be a loose weapon for the attacker.

Figure (1I) The attacker grabs a hold of your wrist on the same side which would be his left to my right, and works the same on the other side, his right to my left. The grip is usually used to pull you forward where he can strike you with his other hand or take your baton.

Figure (2I) Your reaction needs to be quick so as not to let him have a counter-attack. Follow his pulling action, possibly with his hand or fist across your face. As soon as you are grabbed, your reaction should be to step forward, allowing the arm grabbed to go forward as you use the push – pull technique response mentioned earlier in this book. This will give him little leverage to counter by knocking him slightly off balance. This will also allow you to step into the line of danger which is also mentioned earlier. Step into your attacker's pull with your left leg, as you twist your body, bring the left end of the baton up and across the side of his head.

60

Figure (3I) After the shock of being struck on the side of the head as a distract, and your baton is not released, release your left hand on the baton. Look at the picture the attacker is still hanging on **BUT** when releasing the baton, allow it to swing under his arm as shown with the arrows. The baton is now on the outside of his attacking arm and in an upright position.

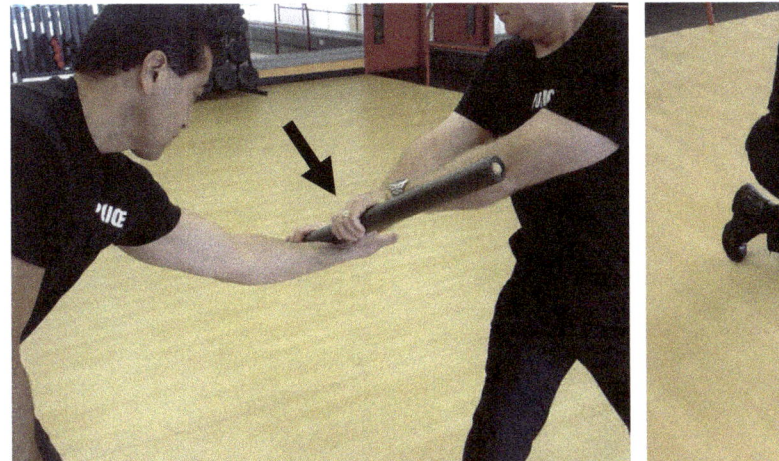 

Figure (4I) The baton is brought over the top of the attacker's wrist and grabbed again with an overhand grip by the hand you released.

Figure (5I) The attacker is pulled forward and down as you step back and kneel. To make this the most secure, his hand is brought down to your knee. The attacker's hand is pressed forward and against your knee, locking it on your wrist and the back of his hand against the baton preventing his release of the baton.

BEAR HUG GRAB AROUND THE BACK
OVER THE ARMS

1J

Figure (1I) When grabbed from the back and around the arms with an actor's hands locked, your mobility is very constricted. This type of situation could occur when an attacker is trying to pull you back or away from a friend that may being placed under arrest.

2J

Figure (2I) Bend at the elbow and bring your baton up above the top of his clenched hands as close to your chest as possible. Now rake the baton down and across his clenched hands to break his hold around you. If needed, you should repeat this motion. With a solid fixed baton or an expandable metal baton, he will release after this goes across his knuckles a time or two.

62

3J

Figure (3J) Once the grip has been broken, release the baton with your weak hand as you grab the attacker's wrist on the same side. Stepping out and back behind the actor, to your weak side, pull the actor's hand away and upward allowing you room to move back underneath. Keep your body upright and not bent over to keep your balance. The step back will lower your height, allowing you to back under the actor's arm without bending over. This also will open the front of the actor to clear your target. The hand holding onto the baton now has a clear target which should strike back against the genitals, lower abdomen, or inner or outer thigh whatever is clear. These targets depend on your step as well as the action from the actor, but one target will be open. The butt end of the baton is used as the striking end as you bring your arm back hard and fast, causing him some real pain forcing him to bend forward.

Please be careful when practicing this technique. Your partner is allowing you to practice these techniques to learn the same as you; not to get injured or see what kind of pain you can deliver. Take care of each other as you would on the street.

4J

Figure (4J) After the attacker is struck with the butt end of the baton, step back under the arm that you are still holding. Do not let your grip slip on the attacker's arm, so when you step back under the attacker's arm, it will rotate the arm forward and his elbow will be back toward you with his arm straight. This position will fall into place due to the attacker bending over because of the strike you have just delivered to his lower extremities. There will not be a matter of having to force the arm into this position with a super grip on his wrist.

The far end of the baton is left in front of the attacker's side or abdomen tightly as you take one more step back with your inside leg. You are now ready for the take down as you have done before.

5J

Figure (5J) As your end of the baton is pushed forward across the triceps, the other end will catch at his waistline keeping him bent over and from standing upright. With your grip still holding his arm straight, you now push forward with the baton and slightly back with his arm pushing him to the ground. When the attacker is forced to the ground, you go down to your knees to prevent you from bending over and in a position that you will lose your balance. Keep some pressure on the baton across the triceps to keep the attacker's shoulder tight to the ground.

To finish this takedown into a submission, bring your inside knee up along side of the attacker's body and over the top of the baton. This will put pressure on the baton and allow you to release your right hand if needed for getting your handcuffs, talk on the radio, or if needed, to defend against a second attacker trying to assist his buddy you have just taken down. The other hand can also be released for a short period of time by bringing you left knee forward and placing it on the attacker's wrist. By taking both of your hands off of the attacker, you will sit up and your balance and pressure will no longer be forward. So be careful in doing both hands for any length of time.

(PLEASE BE CAREFUL IN DOING THIS IN PRACTICE. THE BATON ACROSS THE TRICEPS CAN BE VERY PAINFUL. BE CONSIDERATE.)

CHAPTER 4

ANATOMY STRIKES COME-A-LONG

Anatomy of The Shoulder

There is a little understanding of the anatomy of the shoulder that may give you a better understanding of one of the main baton and cuffing positions. First, understand that the rotator cuff attaches the large bone of the upper arm, the Humerus, to the shoulder joint which is not a complete socket. This is why the shoulder joint is the most complex, flexible and mobile joint in the body. However, these abilities to move in all of the many directions also makes the shoulder particularly fragile. The shoulder joint is really three bones that come together, the scapula (shoulder blade), the clavicle (collar bone), and the humerus (upper arm bone). There are many connecting ligaments, and approximately 20 muscles.

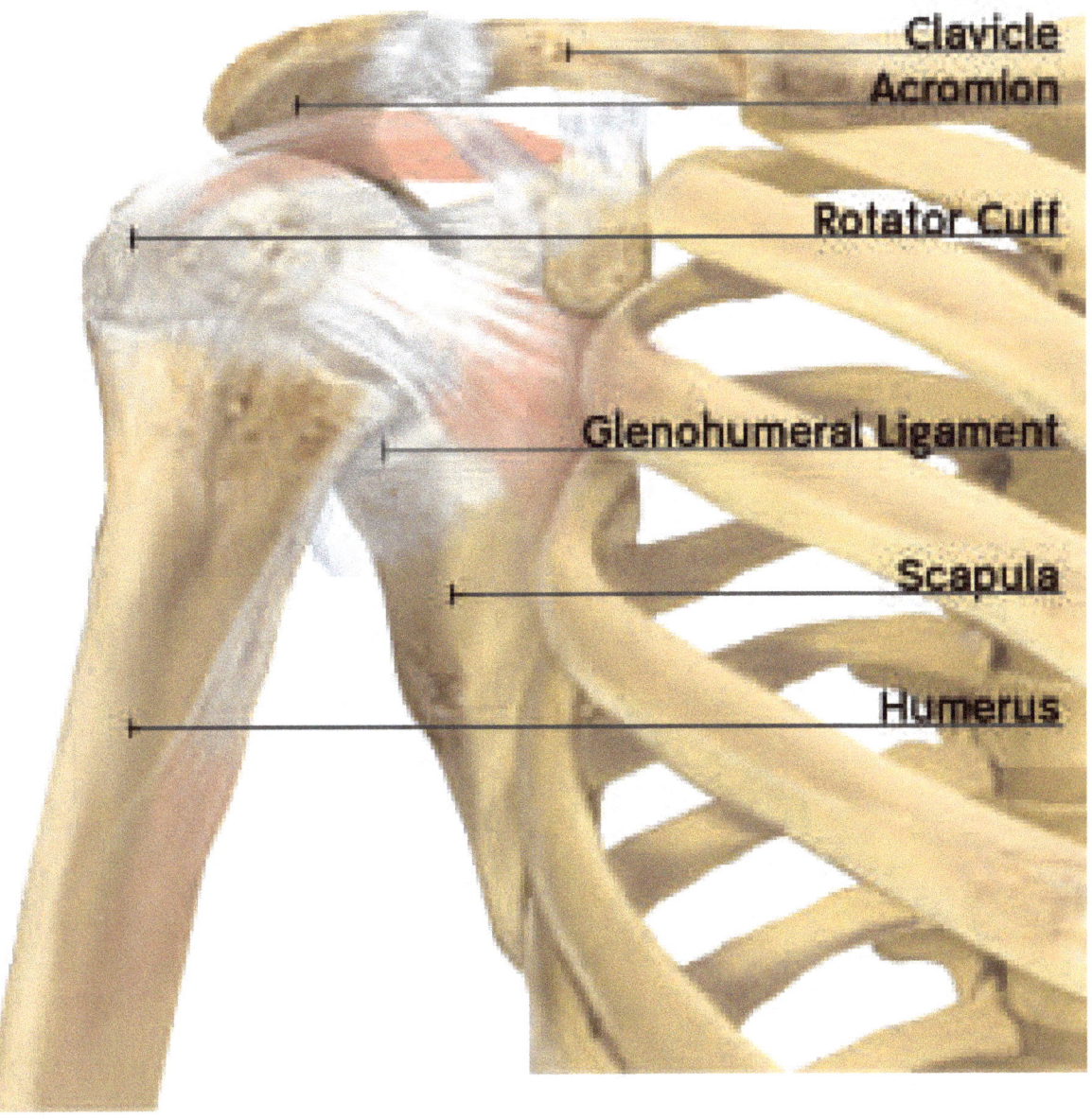

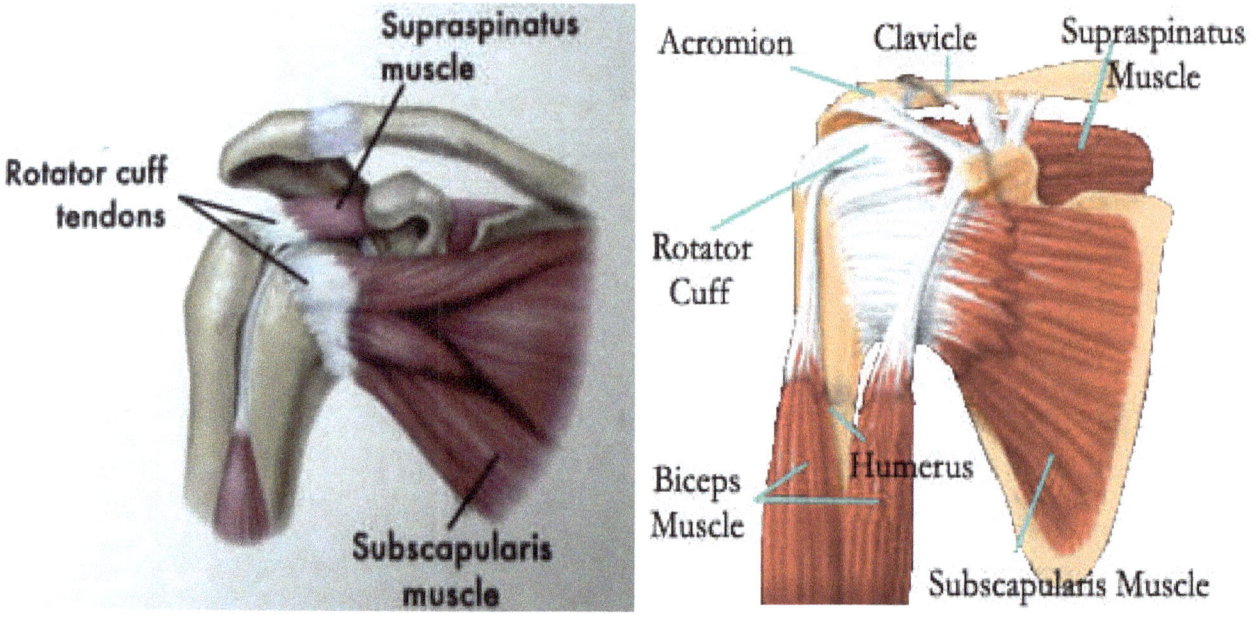

There are only four muscles that attach to the rotator cuff in the shoulder (subscapularis, supraspinatus, infraspinatus, and teres minor). These tendons connect the upper arm bone (humerus) with the shoulder blade (scapula).

Knowing the way that the shoulder is attached, gives us the knowledge of the weakest positions that the arm can be placed to give the least resistance. This knowledge will give the officer an advantage if he is able to place the prisoner in this position.

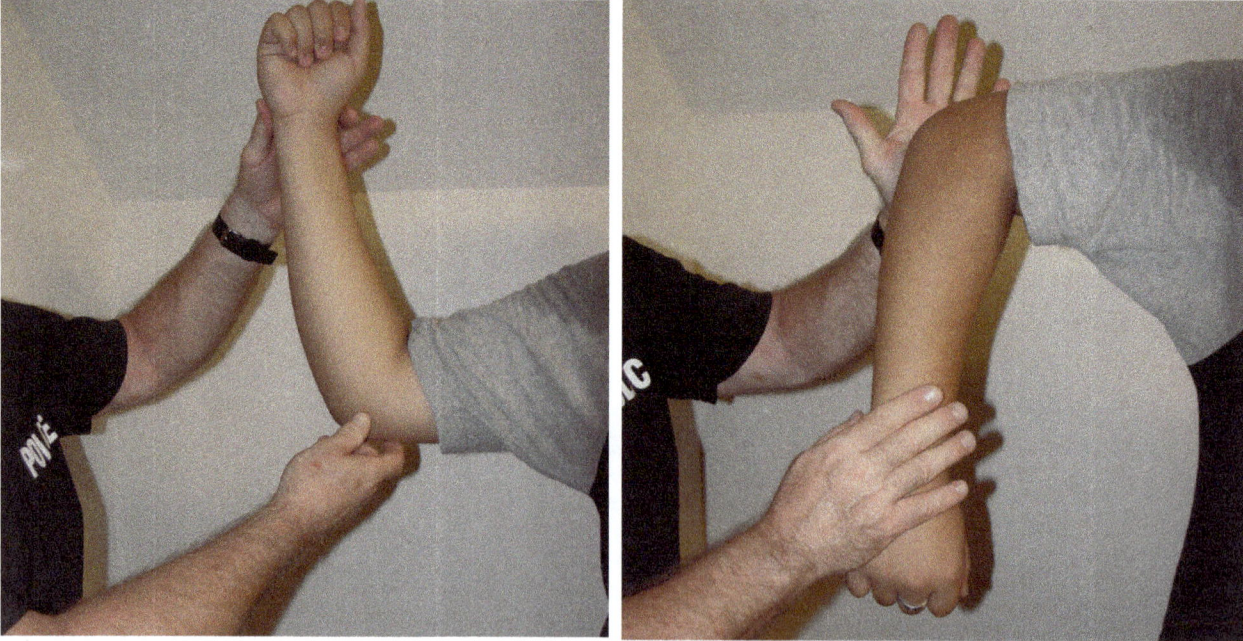

The first picture shows the arm extended out to the side at a right angle in the upward position. The second picture shows the arm extended out in the downward position. These are the two weakest anatomical positions of the arm.

PROTECT AGAINST PUNCH TO THE FACE OR HEAD
(CRUSHING THE DEVIL)

There are actually three motions that cause the breaking down of the front punch with the baton in this section on Crushing The Devil— all having the same result, all effective, and all with the same type of motion on your part. You will also find that the take down after the break down of the punch will be the same.

The anatomy of the arm may help to understand why <u>Crushing The Devil</u> is effective and why the strike is important in the target area.

First look at the structure of the arm. You can see that there are many nerves that run down the inside of the arm between the bicep and the triceps from the armpit area or the axially area of the arm . This is the area that when struck will cause the stunning effect, and even moments of paralyses if struck correctly. The nerves and the main arteries and blood vessels run inside the arm between the bicep and triceps. But, being between the bicep and triceps, it is not protected by a mass of muscle. The most important part of this is that all of these nerves and blood vessels lay over the top of the main bone of the arm, so when struck, causes pain, trauma, numbness, and even a shot term paralysis to the arm that is struck.

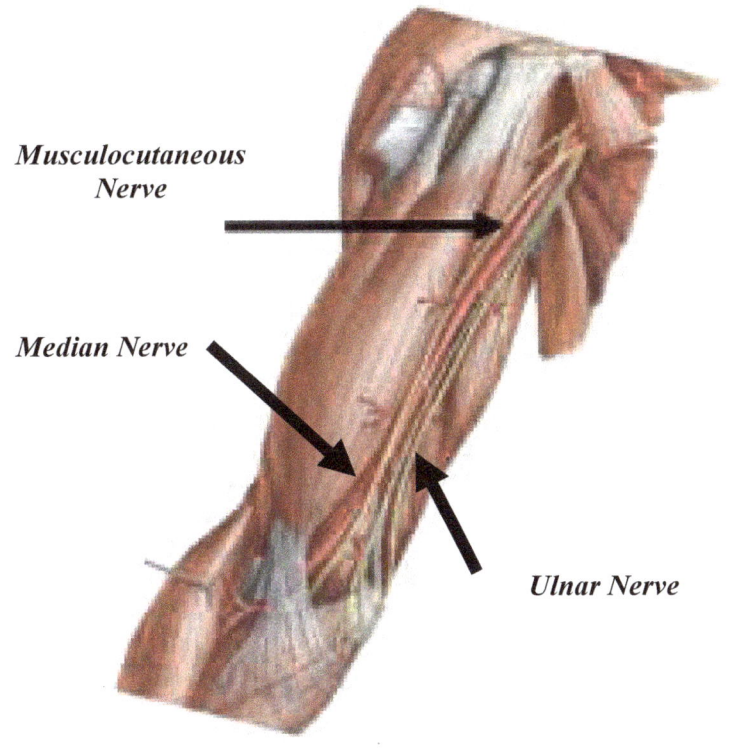

1K

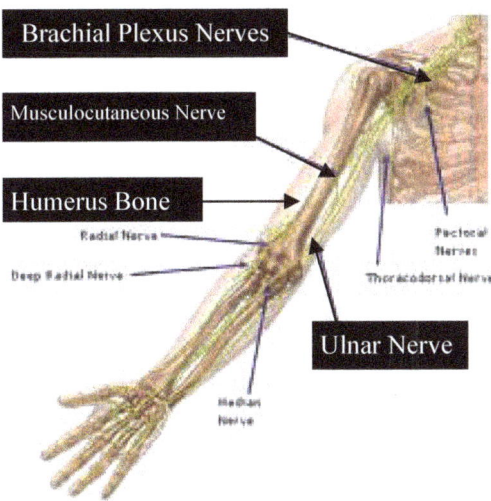

2K

Figures (1K) and (2K)
These are the main nerves in the inside of the arm, that when struck with the baton stuns the arm giving you that extra time you need for the technique

(CRUSHING THE DEVIL)

3K

4K

Figure (1K) The first of the three movements to break down the punch. From a right punch to the face or side of the head, the left hand is released from your baton and used to block the incoming punch. This block will not take the entire blow from the punch. At the same time as the hand comes up to block the punch, the baton is coming across and striking the bicep and inside the attacker's upper arm.

Figure (2K) The second of the three movements to break down the punch the strike is a little different. Instead of the strike with the baton, it is made with the closed hand holding the baton. The same area inside the arm or at the bicep is being struck.

5K

Figure (5K) This is the third strike to break down the oncoming punch. This is the most painful of the three due to the small area being traumatized by the small end of the baton. As the others, when the punch comes at you, the left hand comes up to block and at the same time you respond with a strike with the short end of the baton. This strike uses the butt end of the baton to the inside of the attacker's arm, biceps area, and the Brachial Plexus area. Go back to the chart in this chapter and see the Brachial Plexus Nerve area at the shoulder. These all will cause the most pain and trauma to the area of the arm **BUT** it is the hardest one to perform, because it does take a lot of practice to strike this small area with the tip of the baton.

As said before, be careful in practicing these techniques, and especially this one, due to the striking of your baton, may cause injury to your partner in practice if you are not careful.

6K

Figure (6K) After one of the initial strikes to break down the punch is delivered, the baton is brought under at attacker's arm to the back of his arm and grabbed again by your left blocking hand at the attacker's wrist. This motion is done as you step forward with your outside leg, allowing you to face the baton action.

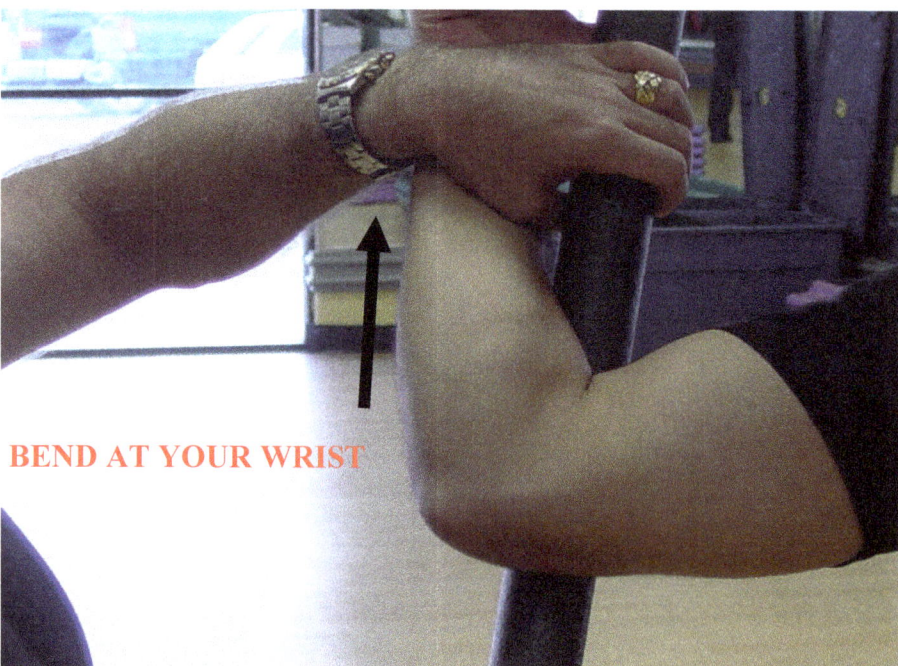

BEND AT YOUR WRIST

7K

Figure (7K) In order for this to be effective, the attacker's arm can not slide out to the side, so the hand that you gripped the baton with at his wrist area needs to now bend bringing your elbow forward in front of his wrist, locking the attacker's arm into place.

This position of the actor's arm is one of the weakest anatomical positions that the arm can be placed in. Look back at the beginning of this chapter and see why this is the weakest position, and you will see a **_great_** reason to be especially careful in doing any technique that places your partner's arm in this position. The shoulder is more fragile than you think.

8K

Figure (8K) When the attacker's arm is locked into place, the baton is turned back pressing down with your upper hand and an upward pull with the lower hand in a counter clockwise direction. This will cause the rotation in his shoulder leading to the take down. Like the other take downs, you need to go down to your knees to prevent you from bending over and taking the chance of losing your balance.

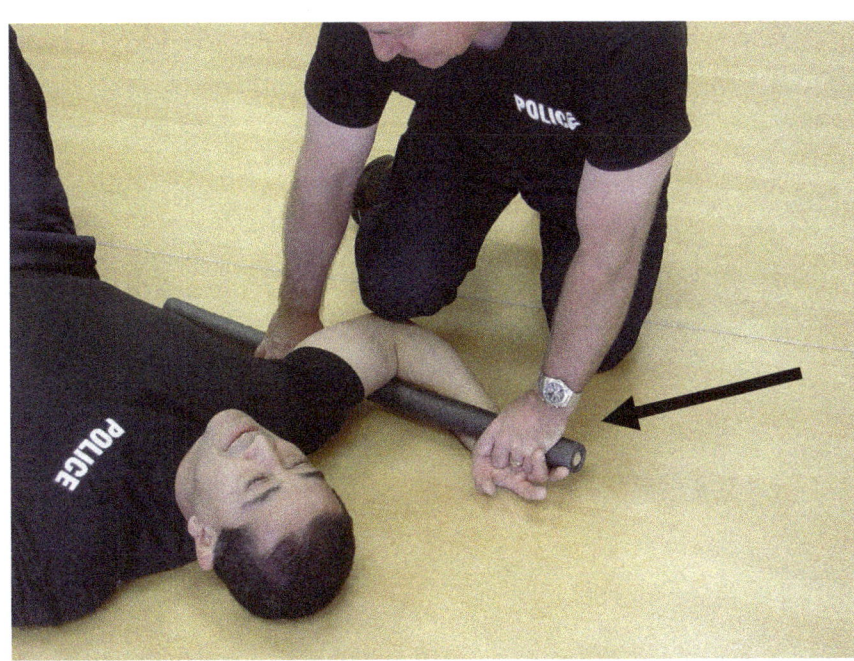

9K

Figure (9K) When the attacker is on his back, adjust the baton so it goes on the top of his wrist, again to prevent his arm from slipping out. To add more pressure to the take down and a submission position, bring your knee up and press down on the end of the attacker's elbow.

(BE CAREFUL WHEN PRACTICING THIS)

SHOULDER LOCK WITH SHORT END OF BATON WITH TAKEDOWN

The break down of the punch here can be the same as any of the three previously used in <u>Crushing The Devil</u> techniques.

1L

2L

Figure (1L) First break down the punch or push using one of the previously shown techniques, blocking with your left hand and strike the baton to the inside of the attacker's arm.

Figure (2L) This time, the short end of the baton is placed over the top of the attacker's arm. Grip the baton with your blocking hand and again bend your elbow so that the attacker's arm does not slip out to the side.

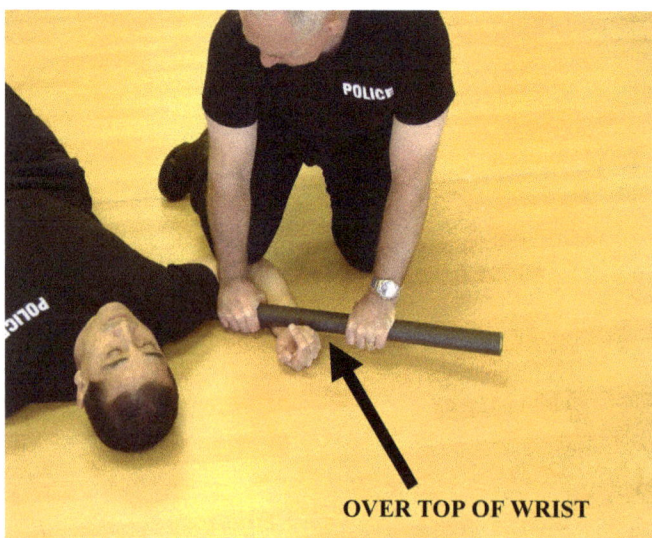
3L

Figure (3L) Rotate the attacker's arm back and to the ground for the take down. Again, reminding you when the actor goes to the ground, you also go to the ground but to your knees, preventing you from bending over and losing your balance. Move the long end of the baton over the top of his wrist, locking his arm to the ground. To go to the submission, the knee is brought up and on top of his elbow. ***(PLEASE BE CAREFUL WHEN PRACTICING)***

ENTANGLING THE ARM FROM OUTSIDE
(*WAX-ON*)

The Wax-On movement is a sweeping movement in front of your face which starts from a movement of the hands from opposite side of the body. What this means is, if you are going to Wax-On going to your right side, your right hand will sweep around in front of you, starting on the left side of your body.

Two main things are needed to have a good and effective Wax-On. First, the Wax-On movement is led with the elbow first. When the arm sweeps to a side, the arm is bent at the elbow, and the elbow comes up across the face and leads the arm in the direction of the sweep, making a circular movement. This movement is not just with the hand, it's the entire arm making the movement. Second, in order to catch a punch or overhead blow, the blow has to be caught. The way it is caught is by cocking the wrist back in the direction of the sweep with the palm toward your attacker.

When using this technique with a baton, the "catching a punch" is easier due to the extension of the baton past the heel of your hand. The notch that the forearm and bent wrist, with the small extension of the baton, makes a larger catching area.

1M

Figure (1M) As the punch is thrown, the baton is brought to the opposite side of your body and moves in a circular motion across and in front of the face as the left hand releases the baton as you step inside the line of danger. The attacker's punch is being caught between your forearm and the short end of the baton.

Left hand reverse grip

2M

Figure (2M) As the circular motion continues to move with the hand holding onto the baton, it will catch the punch and redirect it, and pull him off balance. Bring your left hand under the caught hand of the attacker and grab onto the short end of the baton with a reverse grip. This grip will be "palm facing" you in position. This will scissor his arm between your wrists with the baton locking it in on top.

3M

Figure (3M) The circular motion stops at the bottom, and the actor's arm is trapped. Step back and away from the actor and bring him to the ground. The faster you back up and bring the attacker's arm out in front of him, the easier your takedown will be, he will have no choice. (Use caution in Practice)

SIDE BLOCK WITH HIP TAKEDOWN
AGAINST A FRONT PUNCH

1N

2N

This technique is accomplished from a low ready position where both of your hands are on the baton at waistline. Remember that more speed is accomplished when your arms are relaxed and loose.

Figure (1N) When the strikes starts from the attacker's right hand, your block will be a right block to the back of the attacker's arm as you step in the line of danger, with your left foot. The block will be a low or medium block to the back of the attacker's arm; this means to the wrist or elbow.

Figure (2N) Once the block has stuck the back of his arm and redirected the blow, you should keep the top hand on the baton and release the bottom hand to grab his wrist from underneath. Once you have a grip on his wrist, pull back so his arm does not bend or get away. The top hand on the baton repositions the baton above his elbow to give you more leverage and will straighten his arm. This movement is for only a short period of time just preparing you for the next step.

3N

Figure (3N) To keep the attacker from having time to react to you holding his arm back, the baton is swung down into his abdomen or hip causing him to bend over and bring him off balance and preparing you for the hyper extension of his arm. Two things that have to remain constant at this point. First is your grip on his wrist pulling his arm back and keeping his palm forward. Second is after the strike to the adbomen the end of the baton must stay there.

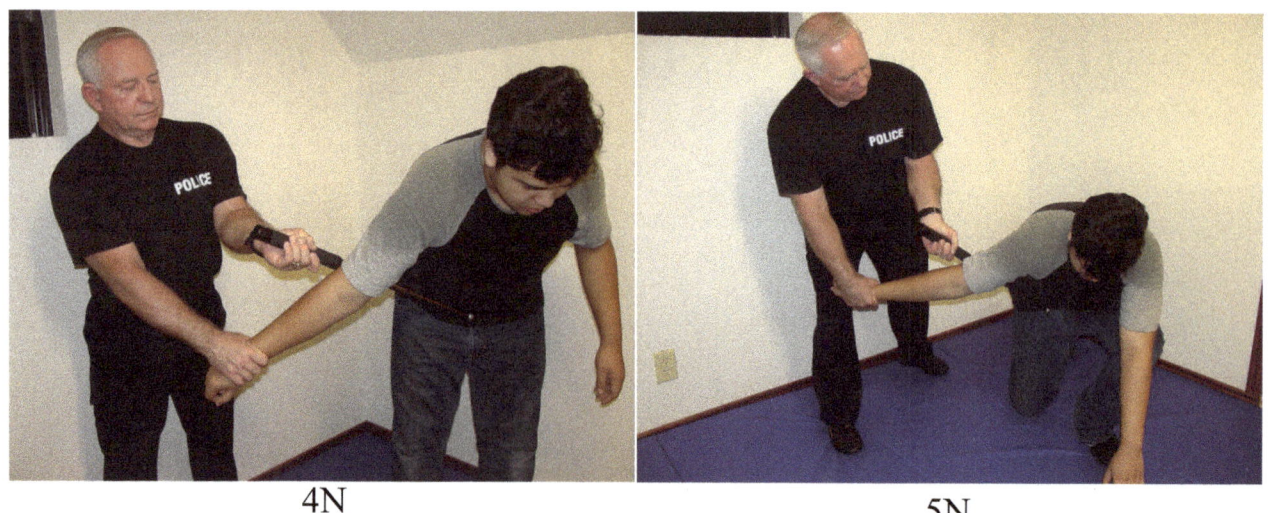

4N 5N

Figure (4N) and (5N) The baton is pushed forward across the attacker's triceps, as the end of the baton remains in the abdominal area. He will have no other choice but to fall forward and place his free hand on the ground to prevent his face from hitting the ground. This is an automatic response to falling forward., which will eliminate him from trying to move the baton from his abdomen or to reach across to assist the arm you have trapped between your grip and the baton. Notice that you step forward with him as he goes to the ground.

6N

Figure (6N) Once your attacker is on the ground go down alongside of him. ***DO NOT BEND OVER.*** This will pin him to the ground. To follow up with a submission and free one hand, bring your inside knee up and place it over the baton, at his armpit area. Applying pressure with your knee on top of the baton gives you the opportunity to release the baton and reach for your handcuffs or get to your radio if help is not on the way. ***(AGAIN USE CAUTION IN PRACTICE)***

SINGLE ARM COME-A-LONG

This technique is a good technique when you have to move a person out of an area such as a bar or where you don't want to start a fight due to the place you are in. Moving this person to a more suitable place to hand cuff or just take him out of the equation. First note that there is an automatic response on his part that happens 99% of the time. This response will assist you in this technique, and as an officer, I know you have experienced it. The response that I am talking about is when you attempt to grasp the wrist of the persons you intend to move or arrest. The second that you reach forward to grab the wrist, **HE OR SHE** will pull his elbow and arm back, maybe even giving the great expression *"DON'T TOUCH ME", or " YOU DON'T HAVE THE RIGHT"*.

1O   2O   3O

Figure (1O) Having your baton out and in your hand in the closed but ready position. When you reach forward and grasp his wrist, the automatic response will start. He will pull his arm back bending his elbow.

Figure (2O) Keep your grip on his wrist allowing you to extend your arm, and him to bend his elbow. When this happens, swing your baton back and down, extending the baton. This is a two function movement. First of course is to extend and lock the baton in place. But the second it also works as a distract when then baton snaps into place. In most cases, the sound of the baton snapping into place delays a secondary turning, or reacting with his other arm.

Figure (3O) Bring your baton forward between his arm and his body quickly. Pulling his arm out to the side slightly.

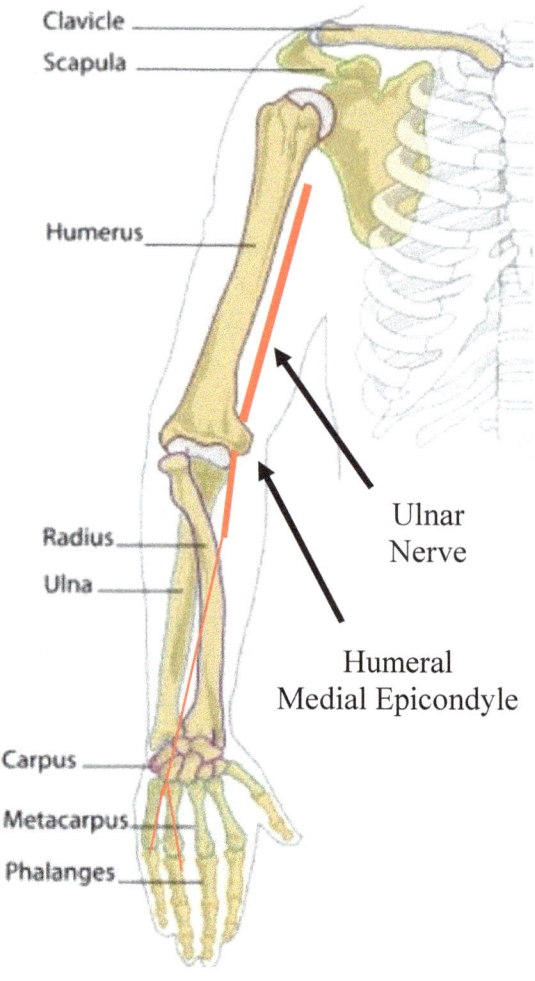

Figure (4O) This picture is to show you what you are striking with your baton. The humerus bone being the large bone in the upper arm, has a protuberance that sticks out at the elbow area called <u>Humeral Medial Epicondyle</u>. The ulner nerve crosses over this bone when the elbow bends, thus exposing the nerve when struck with the baton in this upward motion. The striking of this nerve causes a sharp pulse in the nerve, numbing from the elbow to the fingers.

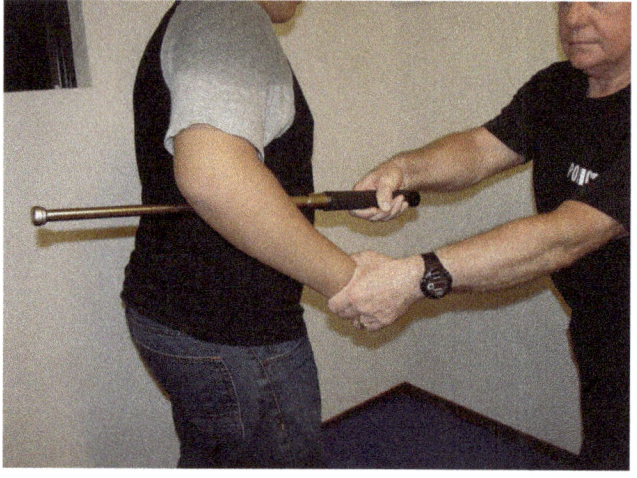

4O 5O

Figure (5O) and (6O) Keeping your grip on the wrist when the actor's arm is pulled back as a reflex action to you grabbing the actor's wrist. The baton strikes the ulnar nerve on the inside of the elbow with the distal end of the baton as the elbow is pulled back. The strike will cause the nerve to numb like an electrical shock, as well as some pain going through his arm all the way to his hand, many times causing the hand to open in a pulsing motion with the shock. This also causes the elbow to pull even further backwards and bend upward Toward the chest. Keep control of the actor's wrist.

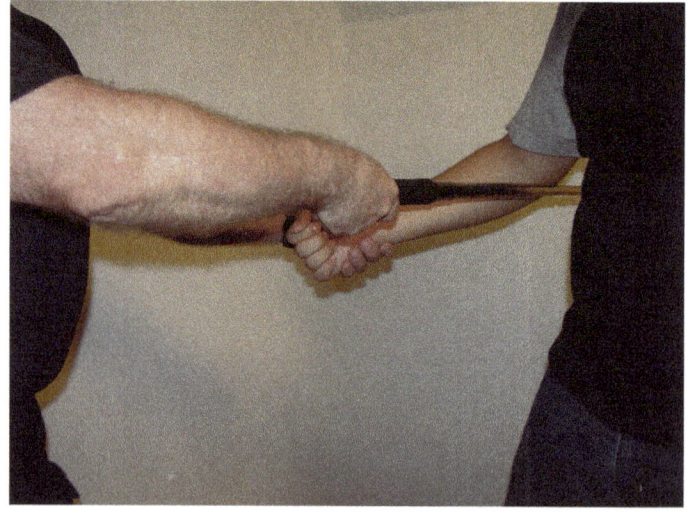

6O

80

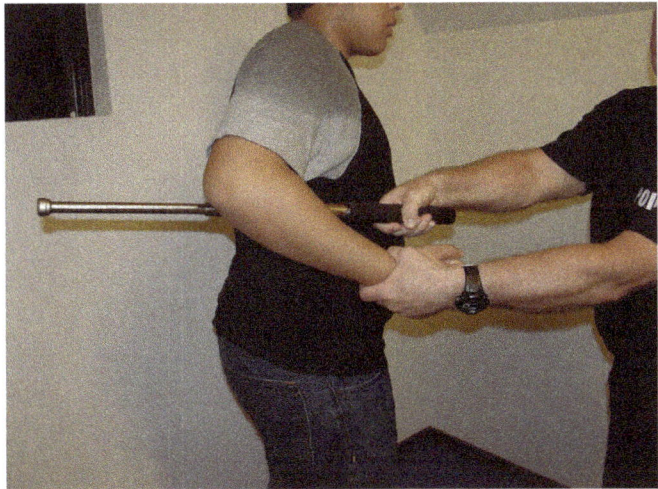

7O

Figure (7O) When the arm bends, allow the baton to be pushed forward about four to six inches further.

Figure (8O) Release your grip on actor's wrist and step forward with outside leg, as you reach upward.

8O

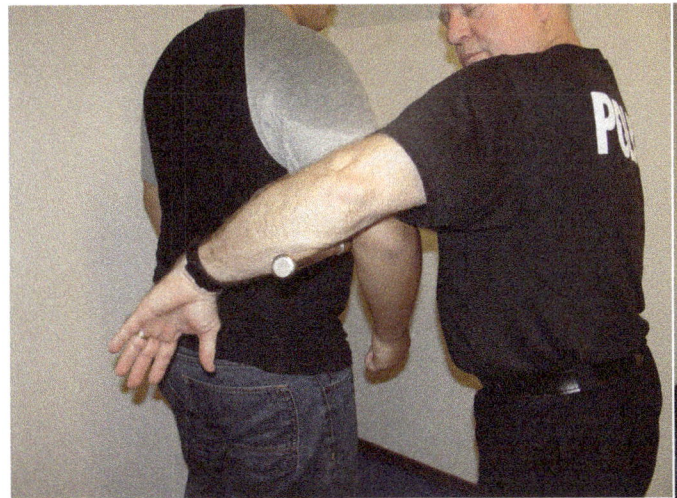

9O

Figure (9O) Reach over the end of the baton sticking out from under actor's arm.

Figure (10O) Wrap you left arm completely over the top of the extended portion of the baton, bending it at the elbow as you wrap around to the outside of the actor's arm.

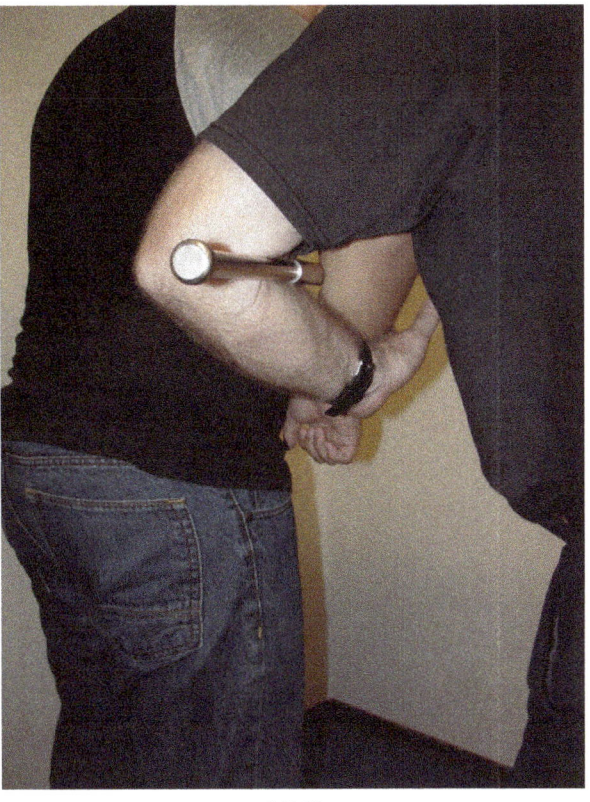

10O

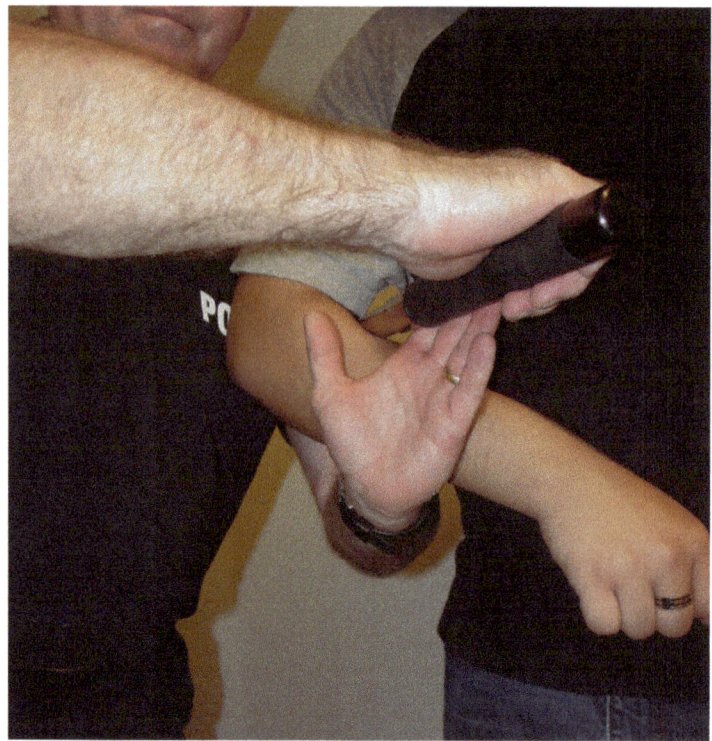
11O

Figure (11O) Wrap your arm under the actor's arm as you push down on the handle of the baton. The metal portion of the baton will put pressure across the radial nerve which will cause pain to the actor's arm.

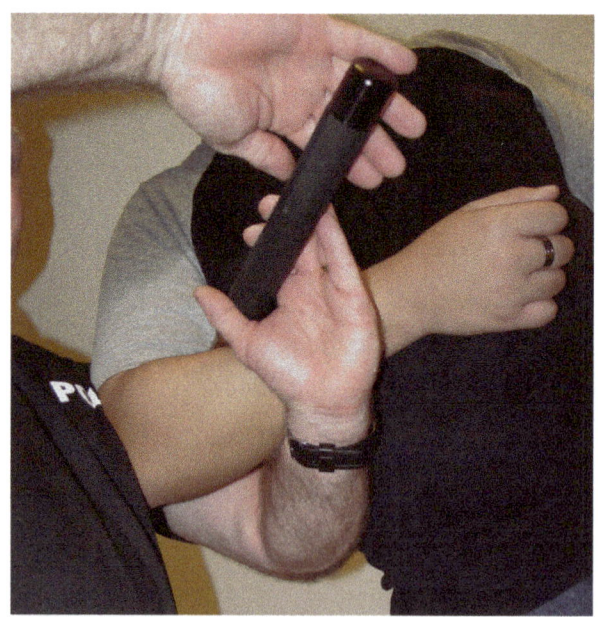
12O

Figure (12O) Reach up with the fingers of your left hand as you push your baton down, so you are able to get a grip on the handle of the baton.

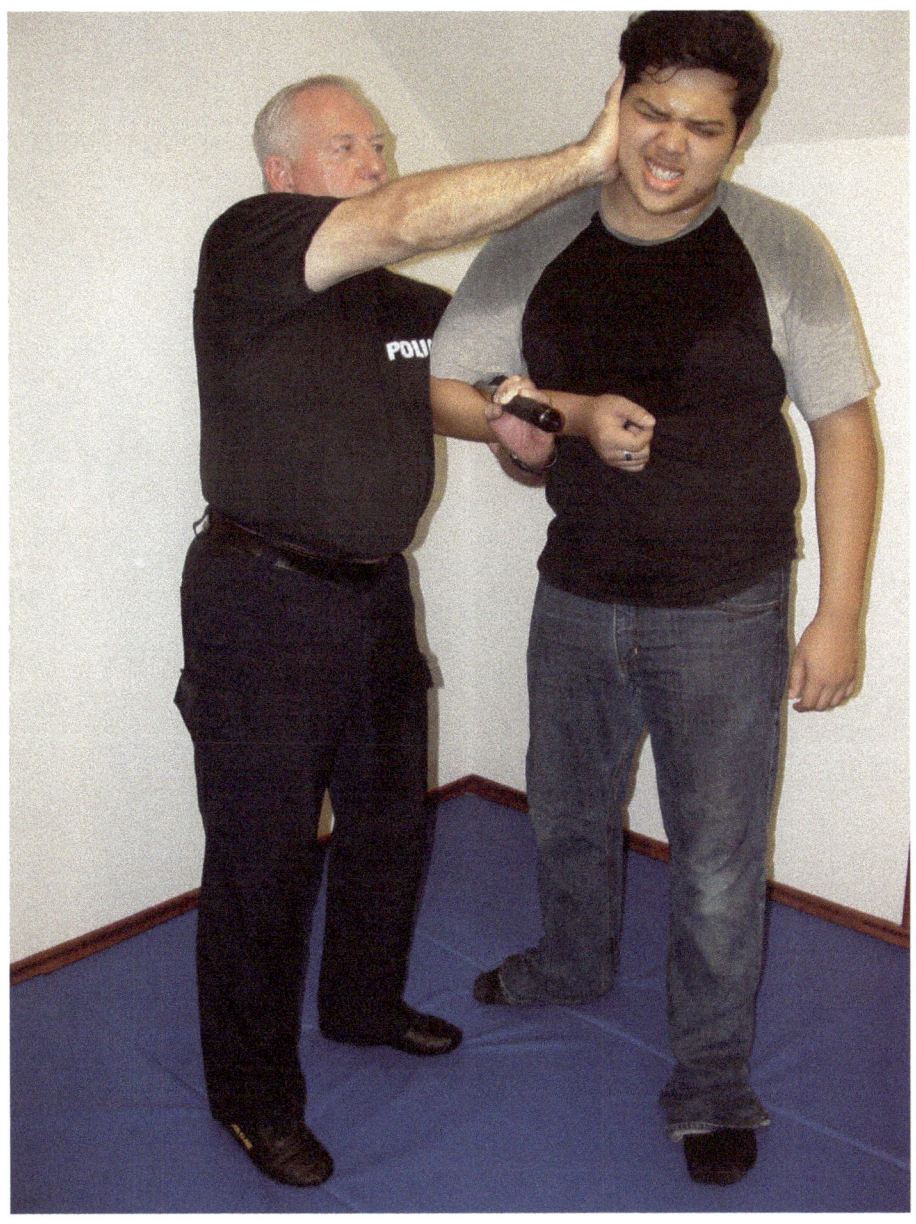

13O

Figure (13O) Gripping down tightly on the baton will put a lot of pressure on the actor's arm and the more pressure you put on by curling your wrist down, the pain will increase. Push the actor's head to the side when moving him so he does not have a chance to spit on you, scream into your ear, or even attempt to bite you.

GARY'S STRIKE
AND TAKEDOWN WITH FIXED BATON

This technique is to protect against a front punch to the head or face with the takedown.

1P

Figure (1P) From the punch to the head, step in the line of danger with your left leg and use the <u>Crushing The Devil</u> technique to block and slow down the punch. Release your baton with your left hand and block the blow from coming in. At the same time, you strike the inside of his upper arm with the baton, while stepping inside the blow. A reminder that this strike to the inside of his arm will stun the arm for a brief moment, giving you the opportunity to start this technique before a counter can be thrown.

2P

Figure (2P) After the arm is struck with the baton, your step with the left foot should be deep so you are standing just slightly in front of the attacker and the arm that you had blocked the punch from. *This next part is important.* The baton is then swung under his arm and placed **behind the shoulder not just the arm**. The baton will be able to move from side to side and forward with the flexion of your wrist, and tilt forward making it possible to place the baton under his chin.

(KEEP THE BATON BEHIND HIS SHOULDER <u>NOT</u> HIS ARM AND HOOK IT UNDER HIS CHIN)

If the baton was placed behind the arm and ***not*** the shoulder you would lose your leverage, and it would be easily pulled out of by the actor. It also would be more difficult to place the baton under your actor's chin due to the angle of the baton.

3P

Figure (3P) Again make sure the hand with the baton is behind the attacker's shoulder. Now that the baton is in position under actor's chin, pull down with the baton to start the fulcrum action by flexing your wrist forward, and straighten your arms and slightly pull the actor to your left side and back. This will give you a little more distance between you and your attacker and start his balance to shift to his right. This will also tighten and lock the baton under his chin so he will not be able to slip his face around the baton.

Lead the actor to his right side by stepping back with your left leg and pulling him to the side with your left arm. This will keep him off balance and bring him into a half circle as his balance breaks down over his right side for the takedown. He will not be able to catch his balance due to the circular movement to his right side and backwards. His left hand will not be able to be brought forward because he is in a fall that is controlled by you. The harder you step back and pull his arm into the circular movement, the harder and faster he will fall.

4P

Figure (4P) Continue your pull on your baton with your right hand, and extending his right arm out to his side until he is on his back on the floor. Keep the actor's right arm over the top of the baton by keeping the tension on the baton. You will be able to release your left hand as soon as you push down on his elbow with your right knee. This will place him in a submission position. This is very painful and take this slow while in practice.
(USE CAUTION ON YOUR PRACTICE PARTNER)

DISCUSSION POINT

There was some worry about this causing damage to the attacker's throat, and possibly damaging the larynx by some departments . The baton will not strike the front of the throat area, it is placed under the chin and the head is pulled back and turned. There is no strike even when done at full speed. After the takedown, when the attacker is on the ground, the baton is at an angle from the neck to under his arm and no direct pressure is placed on the throat area to cause damage to the larynx. The attacker is in a submission when pressure is applied to his elbow with the knee.

GARY'S STRIKE
AND TAKEDOWN WITH EXPANDABLE BATON

There are a few small differences in using a fixed baton and the expandable baton in Gary's Strike and Takedown. Today, most police departments have gone to expandable batons, that is why this technique is good to learn.

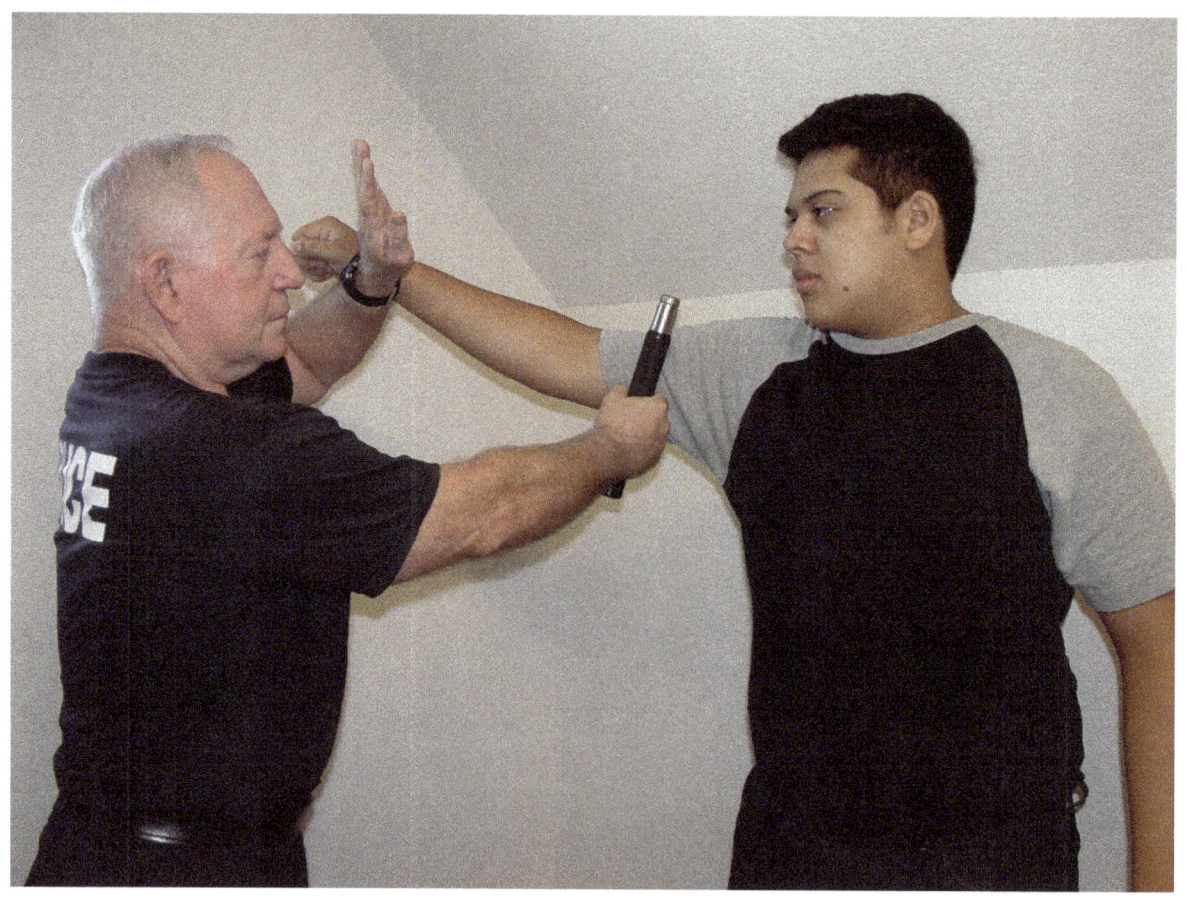
1Q

Figure (1Q) With an expandable baton in hand in the closed position, to respond to the front punch to the face. First step into the line of danger with your left foot, and use the *Crushing The Devil* technique to block and slow down the oncoming punch. As you block this punch with your left arm, strike the inside of the upper arm with the closed baton while you are stepping inside. The strike inside the arm will cause a brief stunning effect to the actors arm, allowing you to do this technique before it can be countered.

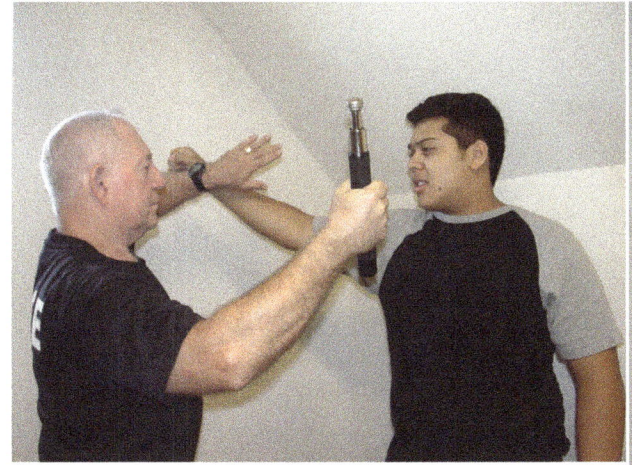

2Q

Figure (2Q) After the initial strike to the actor's arm, the baton hand is brought back quickly with force to expand the baton.

3Q

Figure (3Q) When the baton is brought back, it should be brought back in an outward circular motion to a downward position, so the baton locks into place at full extension when it is at the bottom most position.

Figure (4Q) After the baton has been fully expanded, it is brought forward to the outside of the actor's right leg along the side of his body in an upward swinging motion while the actor's arm is still being held back with your left arm. This positioning is quick, only lasting a split second due to your moving inside; not enough time for response from the actor to counter.

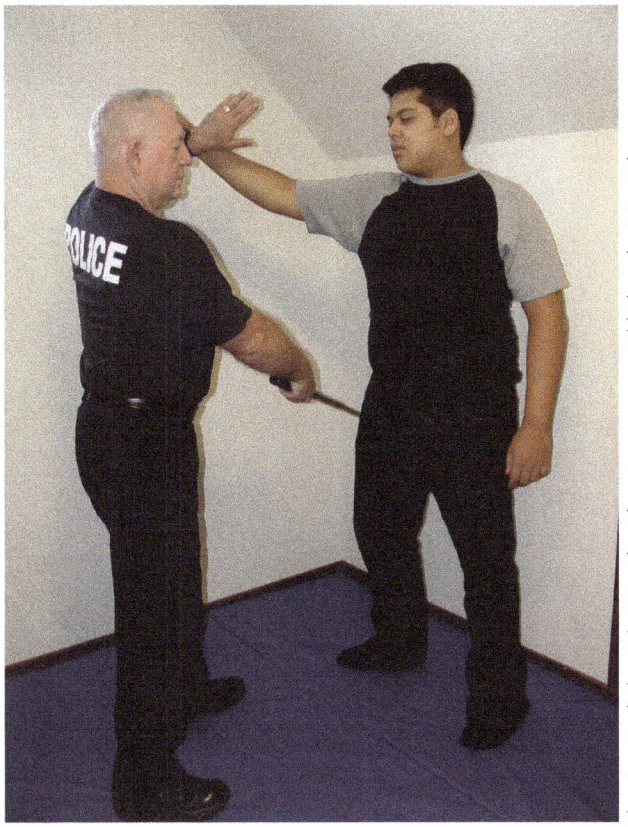

4Q

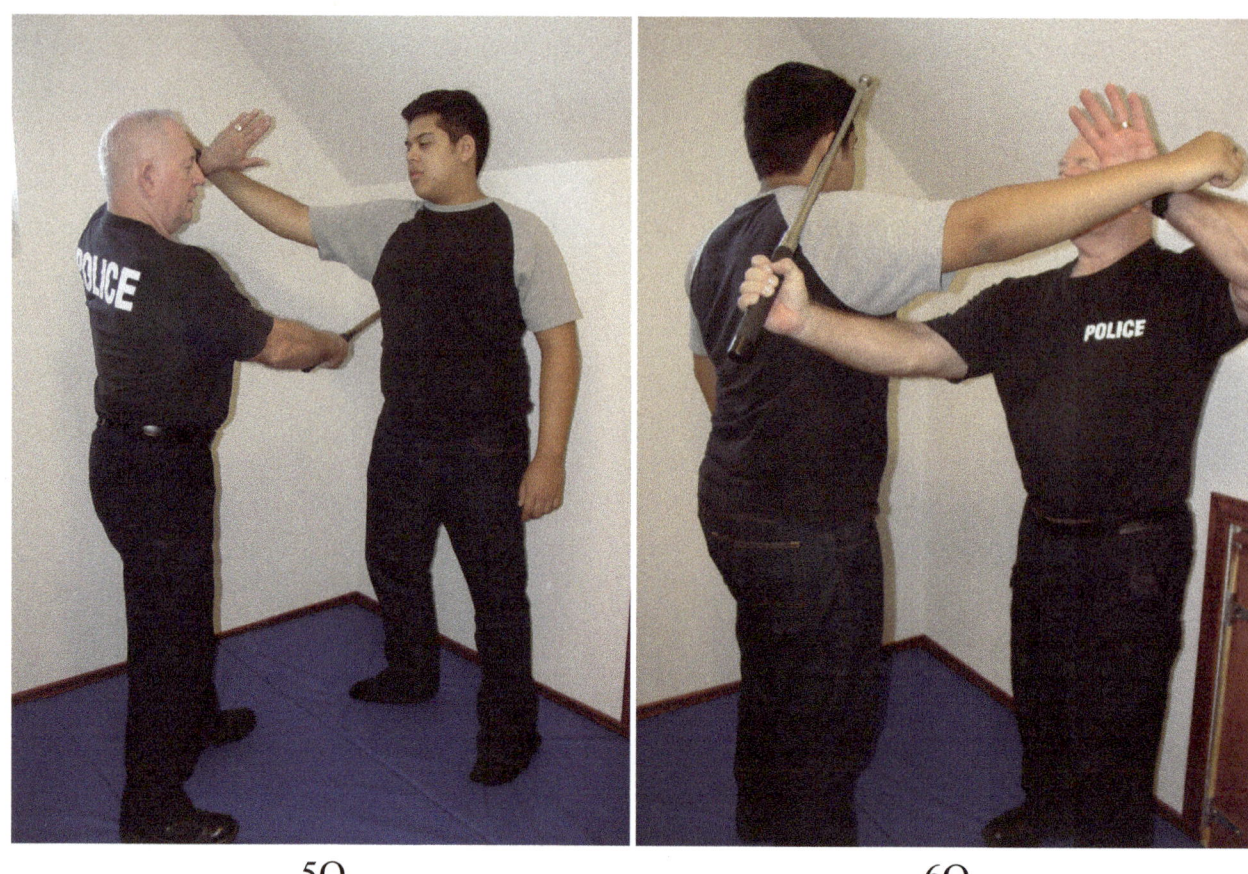

5Q   6Q

Figure (5Q) As the baton is coming up behind the actor, bring your wrist back so the baton comes around his back with the tip of the baton up.

Figure (6Q) When your forearm and hand with the baton come behind the actor, the baton is brought behind the shoulder **_NOT_** just the actor's arm. Tilt your wrist back so the baton comes over the shoulder.

Figure (7Q) and (8Q) When the baton comes over the shoulder it hooks under the actor's chin. Once the baton is placed under his chin straighten the actor's arm. This will increase the leverage of the baton by assisting the baton to lock in place and not slip around the arm as you pull the arm straight and out to the side in a circular motion.

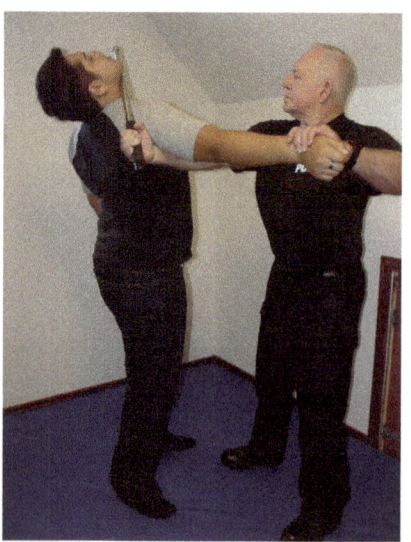

7Q   8Q

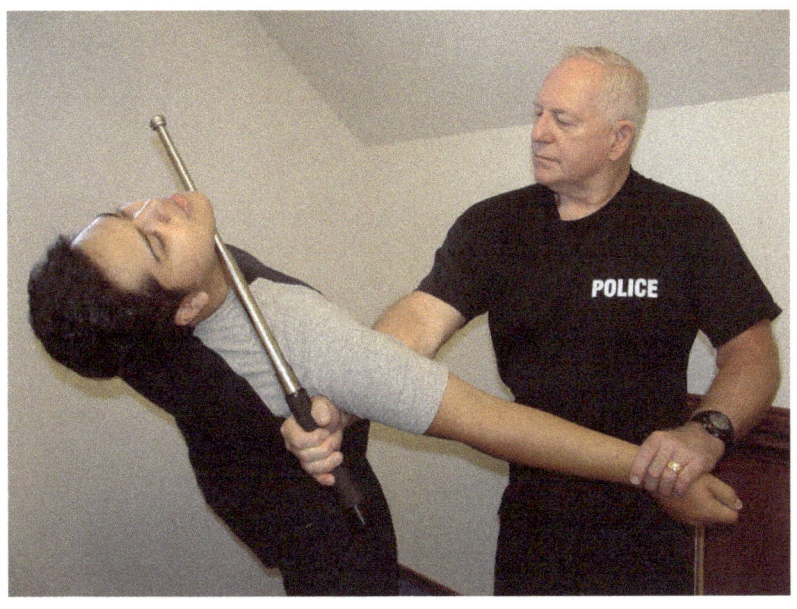

9Q

Figure (9Q) Pull the actor out to the side with the arm you have a grip on. Keeping his arm straight and pulling him to the side will break his balance over his right hip. Pulling back on the baton will tilt his head back also causing him to lose his balance. His balance has to be controlled to the side over the right hip, so he does not just fall straight back onto his head and cause injury. Remember the body goes where the head goes.

<u>*When in practice, take it slow.*</u>

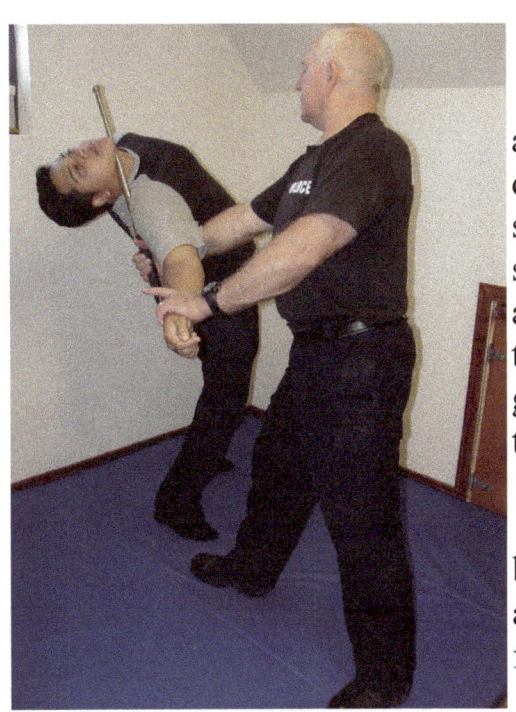

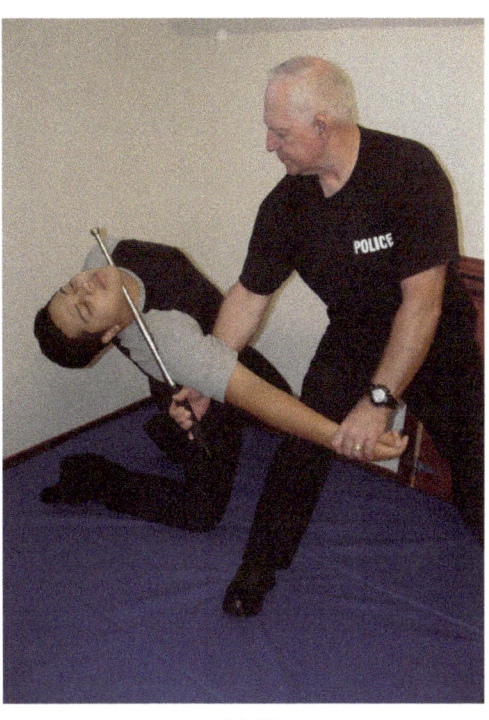

Figure (10Q) This shows the actor being drawn out to the side, now straightening the arm that the baton is in, to get a good lock under the actor's chin.

Figure (11Q) The balance is broken over the actor's right hip for the takedown.

10Q   11Q

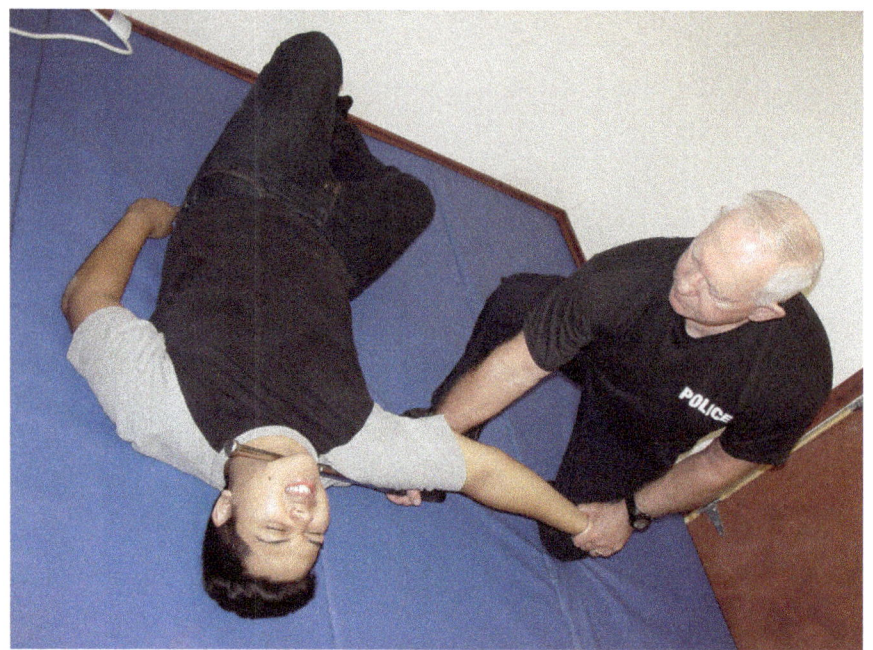

12Q

Figure (12Q) When the actor is down and on his back, keep your baton behind his shoulder. This does not cut off his airway, and in most cases the actor will turn his head which eliminates the probability to cause injury to his trachea.

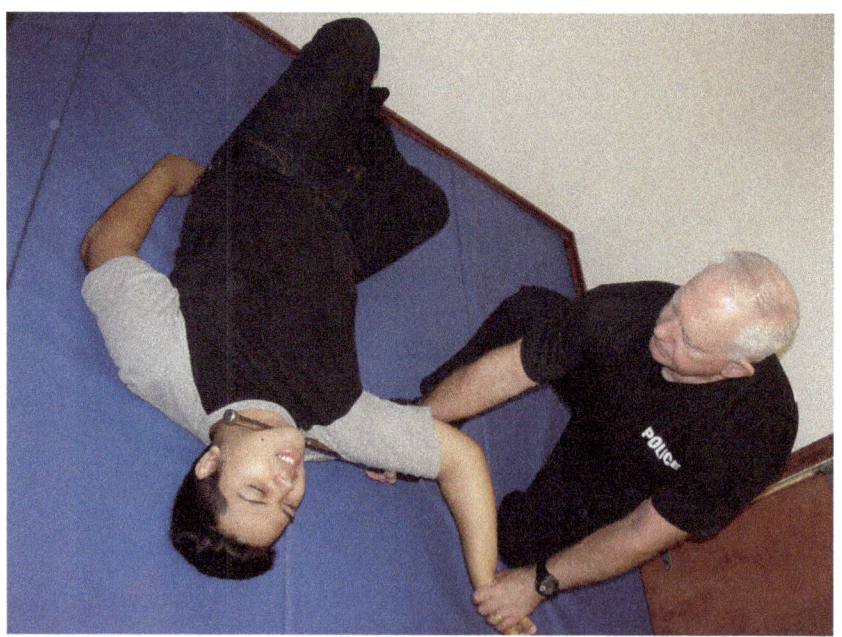

13Q

Figure (13Q) As I mentioned in the previous picture, the actor will turn his head to the side preventing any kind of throat injury. If keeping your actor in this position for any length of time, bend his elbow and kneel on his wrist or elbow.

BONUS

VEHICLE EXTRACTION WITH BATON

BATON HYPEREXTENSION VEHICLE EXTRACTION

This extraction with the baton is a bonus to this book coming from the Police Bujitsu Club Vehicle Extraction Course. This is an excellent extraction that can be used when an actor is not compliant and refuses to exit from the vehicle.

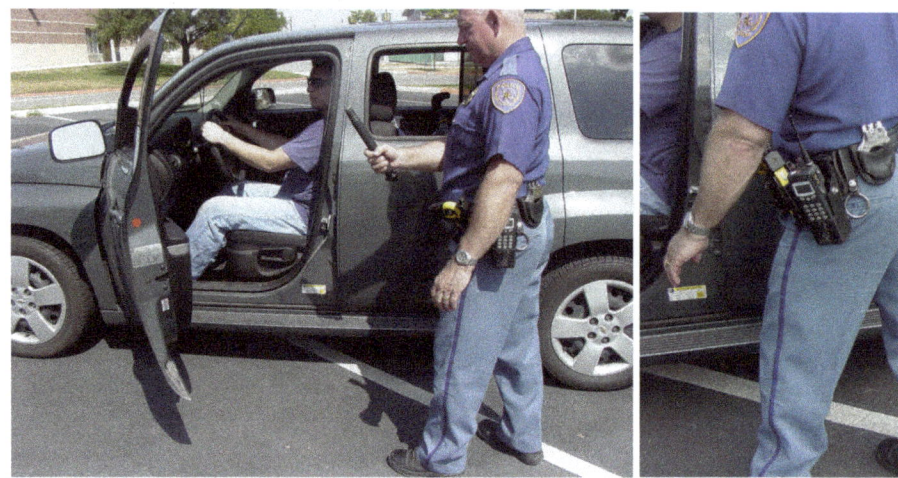

1R

Figure (1R) When you approach the vehicle, open the driver's door. If possible, try to have him remove the seat belt. If you can't remove the belt, it should be done after he is under control by another officer. We'll let you know when we get to that part. Draw your baton, whether fixed or expandable. This extraction will be done with an expandable baton. Here longer is better as batons go.

Figure (2R) Extend your baton with a quick snap down to your side to make sure it locks firmly in the open position, so it will not collapse when being used.

Figure (3R) Bring your baton forward changing your grip on the baton from a thumbs down to a thumbs up position in your right hand. This grip will give you a stronger grip and control over your baton which is needed in this extraction. The grip with a fixed baton will be the same, in the thumbs up position.

3R

94

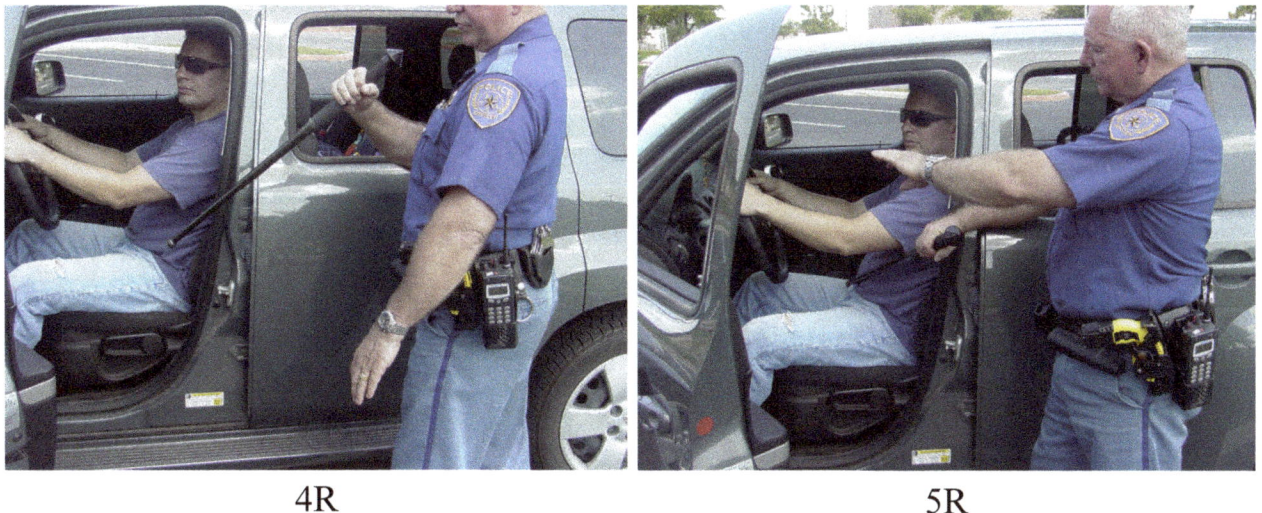

                4R   5R

Figure (4R) When your grip is secure bring the distant end of the baton forward

Figure (5R) Place the end of the baton under the driver's arm and to his lower abdomen area or belt line, and if possible place the end of the baton inside his belt. Bring your left hand up directing the driver to extend his left hand out of the vehicle. This will allow you to be ready if the hand does come quickly.

                6R   7R

Figure (6R) Reach forward gripping his wrist so your fingers are over the top of the wrist and your thumb around his wrist to assist his arm toward you and keep it extended. This will also prevent his arm from rolling forward trying to

Figure (7R) At this point, he may not release the steering wheel, and become more uncooperative. Make sure your grip is tight at his wrist, keeping the baton at the belt line and press forward with the baton as you pull back at his wrist. He will release his grip or lean forward against the steering wheel.

SEAT BELT RELEASE

If he did or did not release the steering wheel, this is where you would pause to have another officer release the seat belt from the other side, if the actor would not take it off previously.

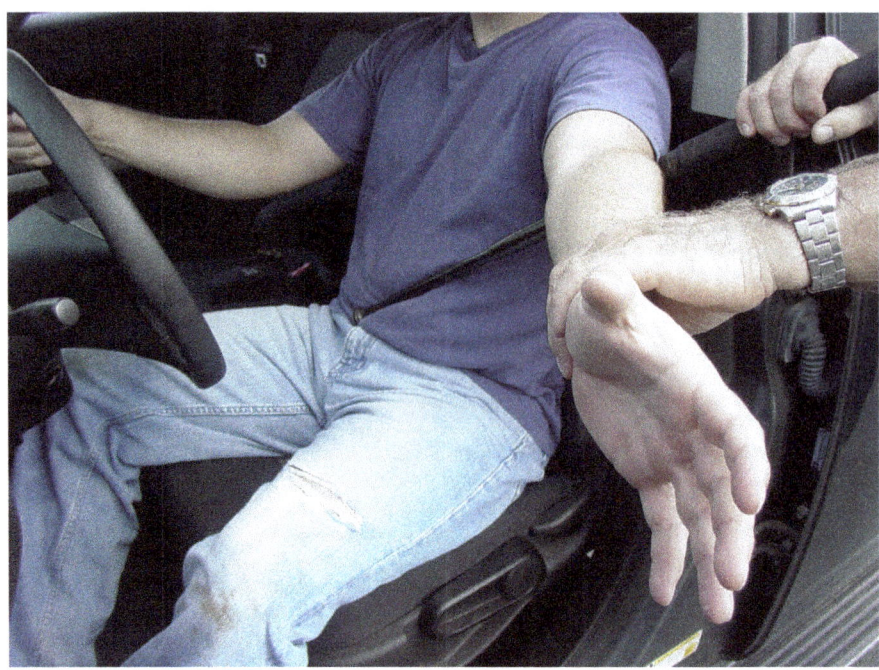
8R

Figure (8R) Make sure the actor's hand is palm forward and the arm is straight. The baton is at the belt line at the distal end and the other end is placed across his triceps above the elbow. There is no need for a lot of pressure to be applied with the baton. Use as much pressure as needed to show control allowing him to cooperate as he sees fit, you're in control now.

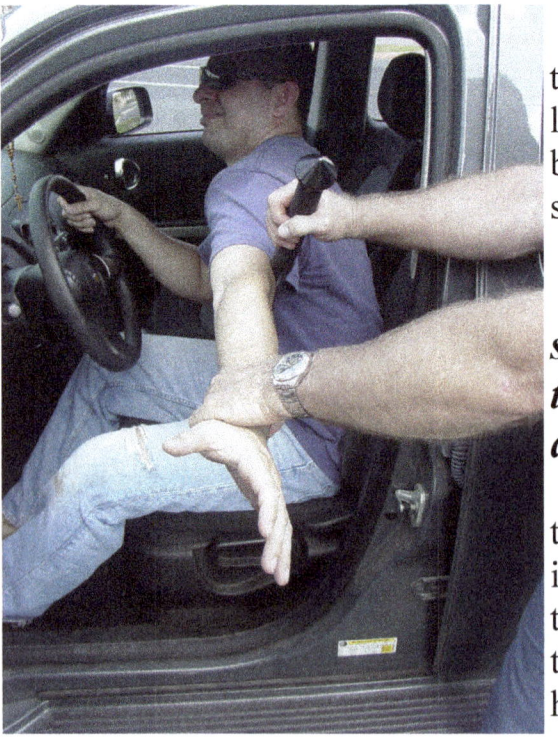
9R

Figure (9R) Pressing forward with the baton causes the baton to tighten at his waist line. If you were able to place the end of the baton in his belt, it will prevent it from ever slipping around the stomach area.

When you have persons with large stomachs, the baton will set over the top of the stomach, closer to the chest area.

When you press the baton forward, the baton will be tight up across the triceps, and this is painful. The first reaction is for the actor is to roll his shoulder forward and lean toward the steering wheel. This will make sure that his arm is in the correct place and in a locked position.

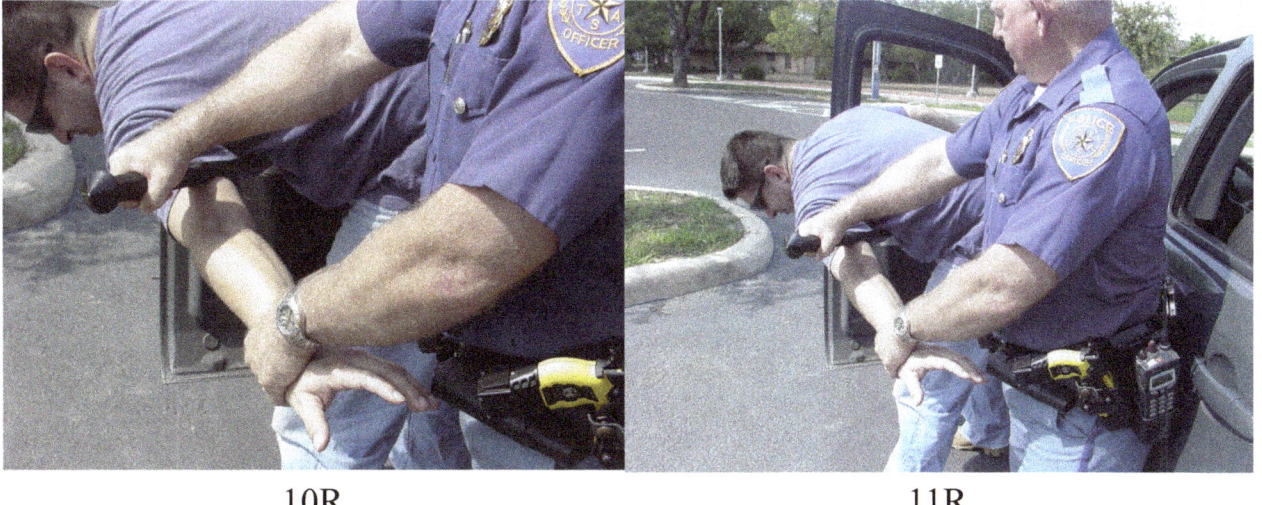

10R   11R

Figure (10R) and (11R) Once the baton is tight against the triceps and the arm is locked, lead the actor out of the vehicle by pulling the actor's arm with your left hand. Press forward with the baton keeping the baton tight against the triceps as you move the actor from his seat in the vehicle. When the actor first steps from the vehicle, take it a little slower and give him time to allow him to get his feet on the ground. Being in a leaned over position, he will want to go to the ground on his face. If the vehicle is high and he has to step down to the ground, make sure that both feet are on the ground before going any further. If the vehicle is low, get him to stand up on both feet, but still leaned over.

12R   13R

Figure (12R) Keep pressure on the triceps and the baton will stay at his waistline as you push forward with the baton and pull back slightly with his arm to lead him away from the vehicle.

Figure (13R) When you are ready to place your actor on the ground in an area you feel comfortable with, just pull his arm back and push him forward to the left.

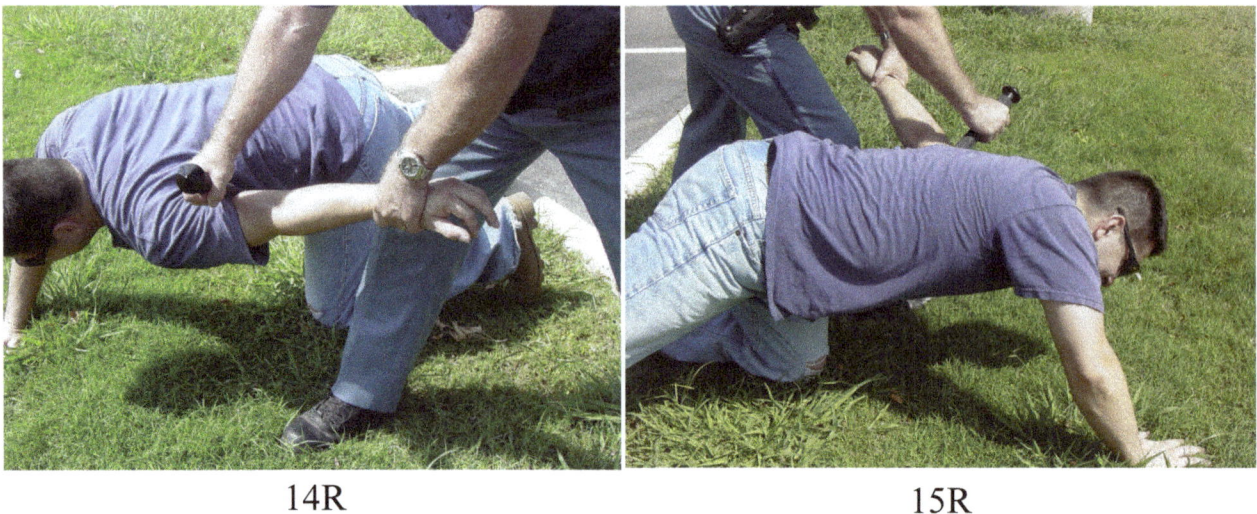

14R   15R

Figures (14R) and (15R) Pushing your baton forward and pulling the arm and his body away from his support hand, this will not allow his support hand to come across and catch his balance. The momentum of the entire action of pushing on the baton and pulling his body to his weak side will cause him to dip his shoulder to the ground and lay flat.

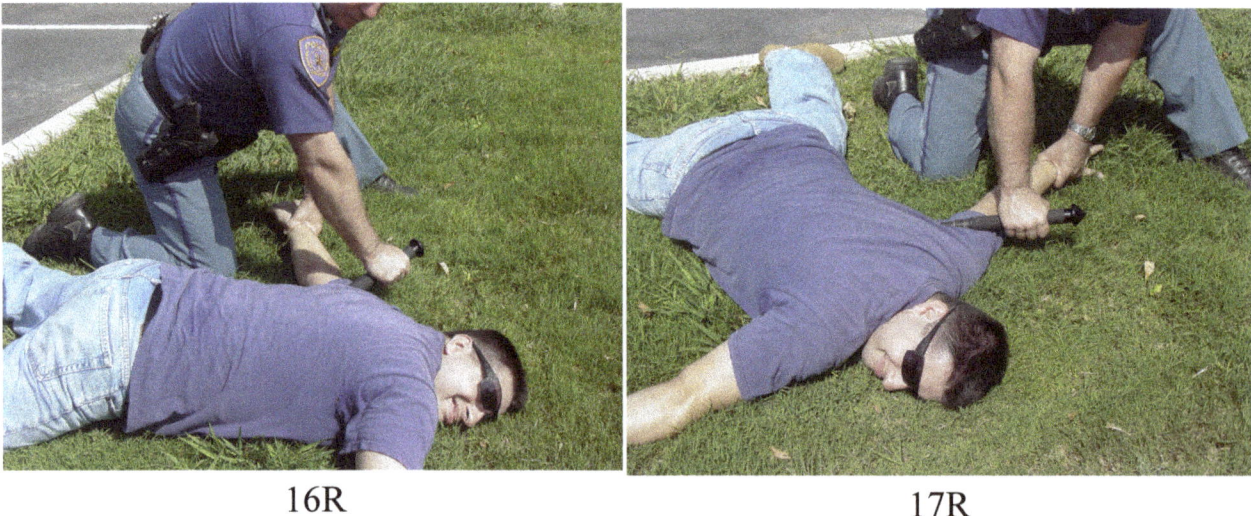

16R   17R

Figures (16R) and (17R) When he lays flat on the ground, the baton stays across his triceps. Have the actor turn his face away from you. Kneel down along side of the actor to prevent you from bending over and losing your balance or cause you any back strain. Keep his arm extended to the side, not allowing it to bend nor come back to his side. When you actor is in this position, it is a submission position. This will allow you time to wait for support and also give you time to look around, making sure that there are no friends or cohorts close to give your actor some help.

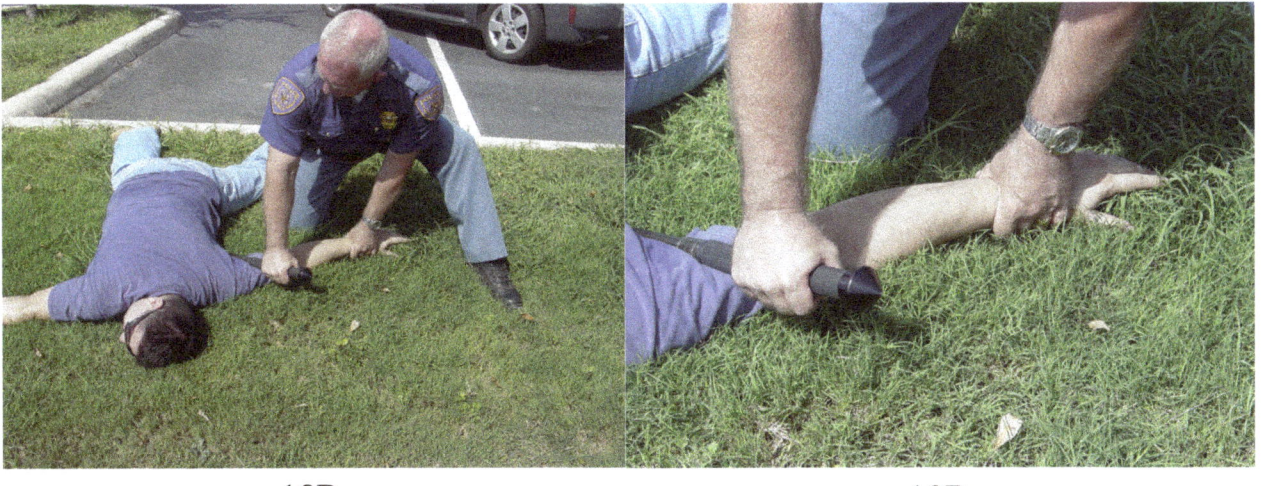

18R 19R

Figures (18Q) and (19Q) Once your actor is laying face down, you have total control and time to switch your position. Lean forward, keeping the pressure on your baton and his arm out to the side and his palm down.

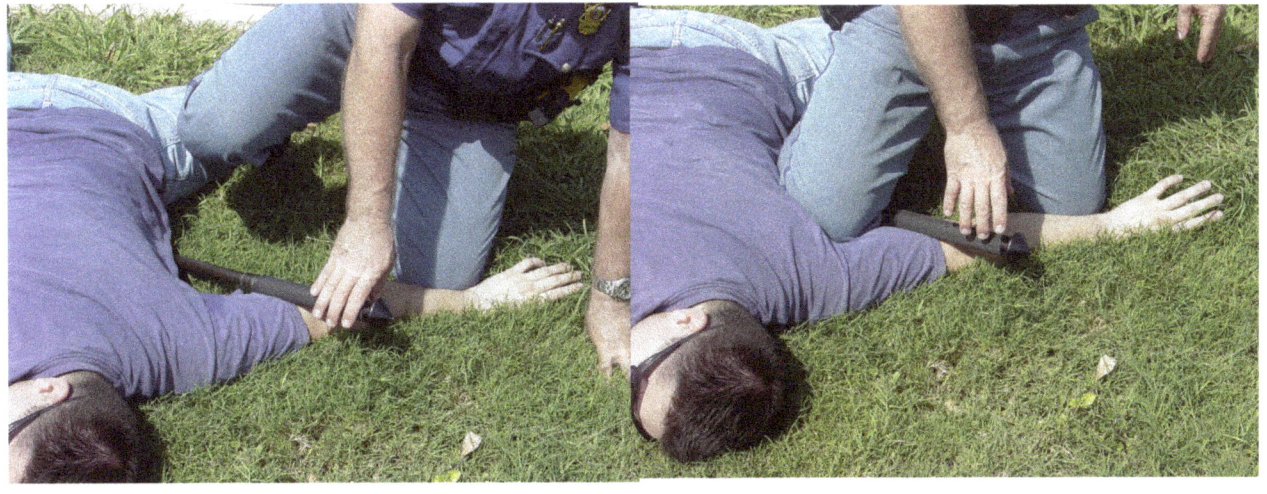

20R 21R

Figure (20R) Move your outside knee back behind the wrist and forearm preventing the actor from bringing his arm to his side. Bring your inside knee up. Note that all your weight is not just on the baton. If all your weight were placed on the baton when shifting position, this would be extremely painful to the tricep area of the actor's arm. **In practice, be careful not to injure your partner.**

Figure (21R) Place your inside knee across the baton into the space between his body and the baton, and allow your shin to rest on the baton. This will keep the baton in place, and your actor still in the submission position. Remember placing your weight on the baton is painful, be considerate when practicing with your partner.

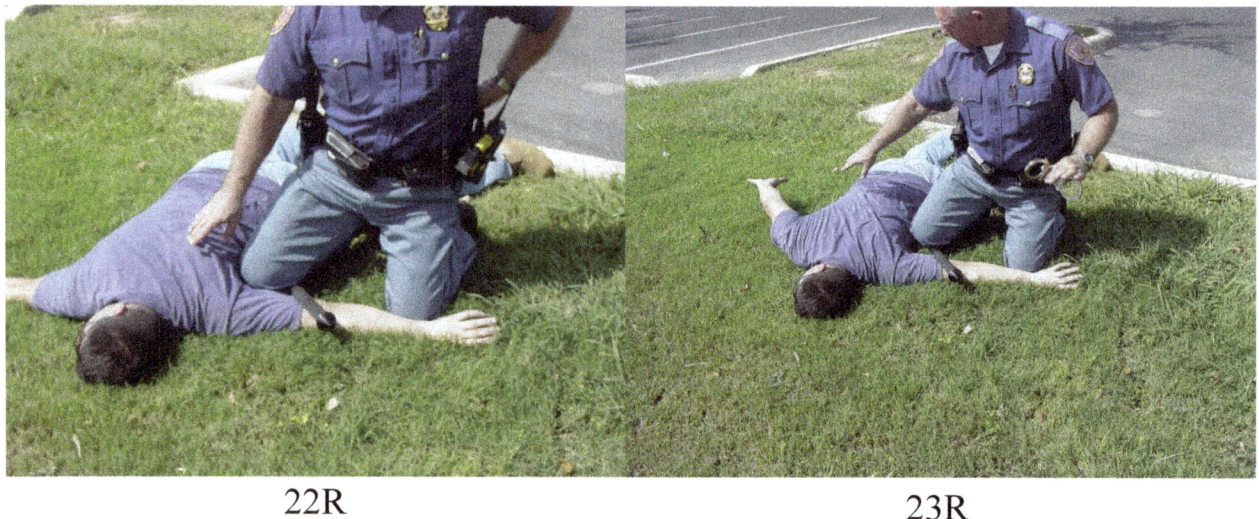

22R 23R

Figure (22R) Now your baton is secured with your knee, both of your hands will be free to use your radio or reach for your handcuffs.

Figure (23R) When the decision is made to handcuff your prisoner, direct your prisoner to place his hand back across his back, as you draw your handcuffs from their pouch. Place your handcuffs in your hand so that the ratcheting side of the cuff is forward toward your prisoner.

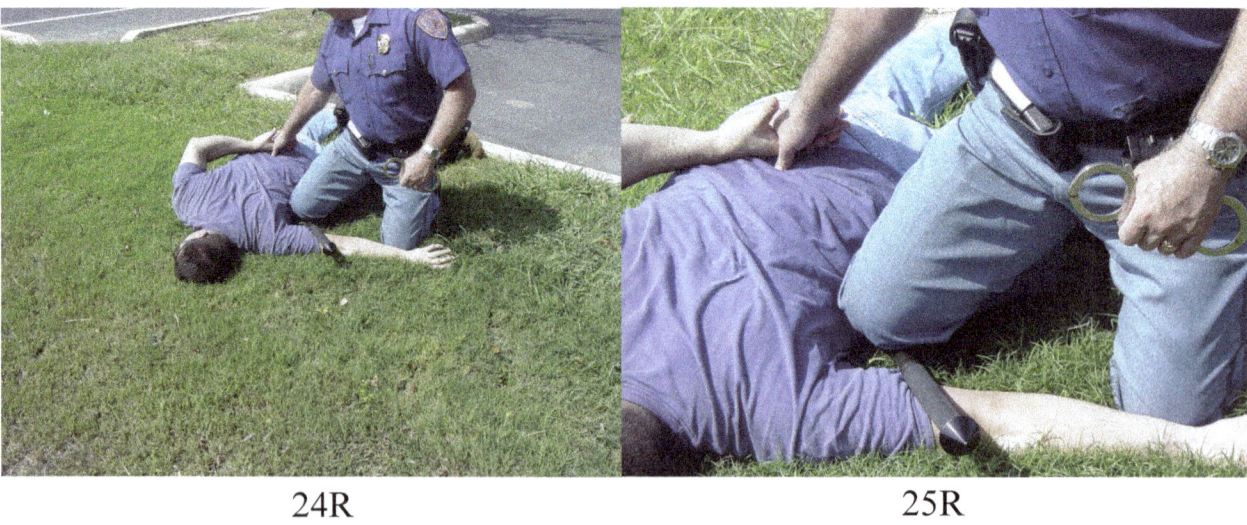

24R 25R

Figure (24R) Keeping your balance back over your hips, make the actor bring his hand back to you so you are not reaching and become off balance. Grip the fingers of the actor's hand.

Figure (26R) Now you are ready to place him in handcuffs, keeping your weight on the baton, your balance over your hips, and a good finger grip.

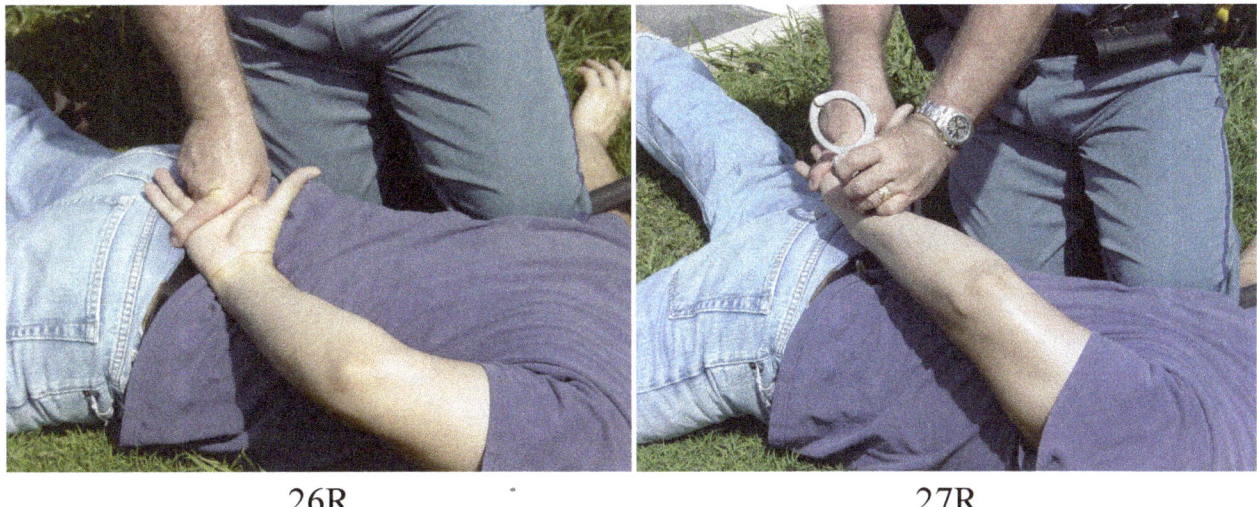

26R 27R

Figure (26R) Keeping the hand and arm under the baton with your weight on your knee, face toward the actor getting a grip on his hand as it comes back to you upon your request. Pull his hand and arm across to mid back so you are not leaning to reach over the top of his body.

Figure (27R) Place the bottom cuff on the actor's wrist first. With the grip on the actor's hand, turn his wrist back toward the heel portion of his hand. This will help prevent the wrist from bending and trying to get a grip on your hand as you place the handcuff on ratchet side forward.

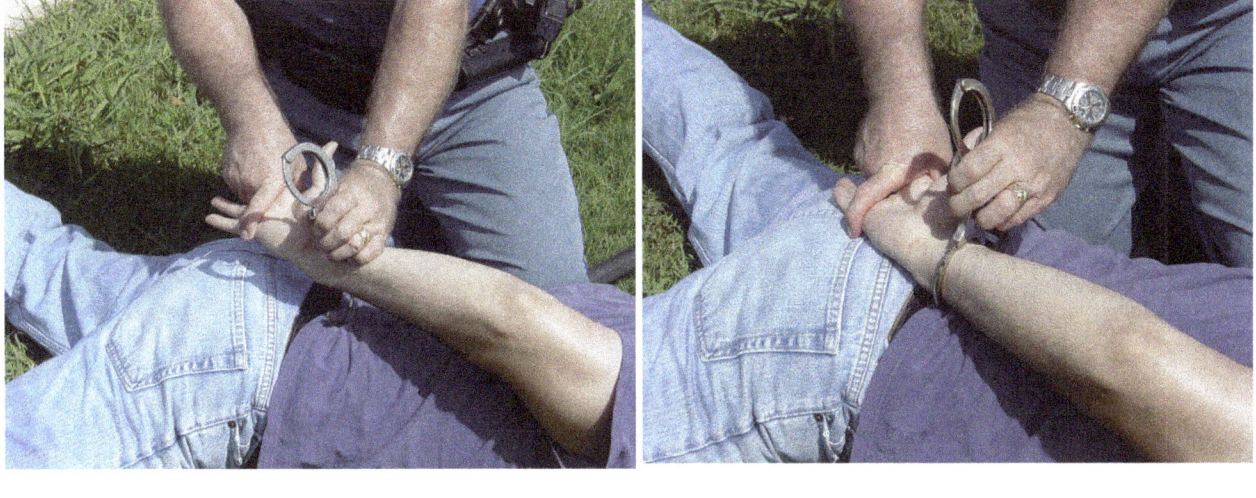

28R 29R

Figure (28R) When the handcuff is applied to the actor's wrist, lift his hand up and away from his clothing so as not to snag the ratcheting end of the cuff on his clothing.

Figure (29R) Make sure that the handcuff clicks into place as you push the cuff forward with your left hand and pull his wrist up against the cuff with your right hand.
(This works best with Hinge or Ridged cuffs as they do not spin on you.)

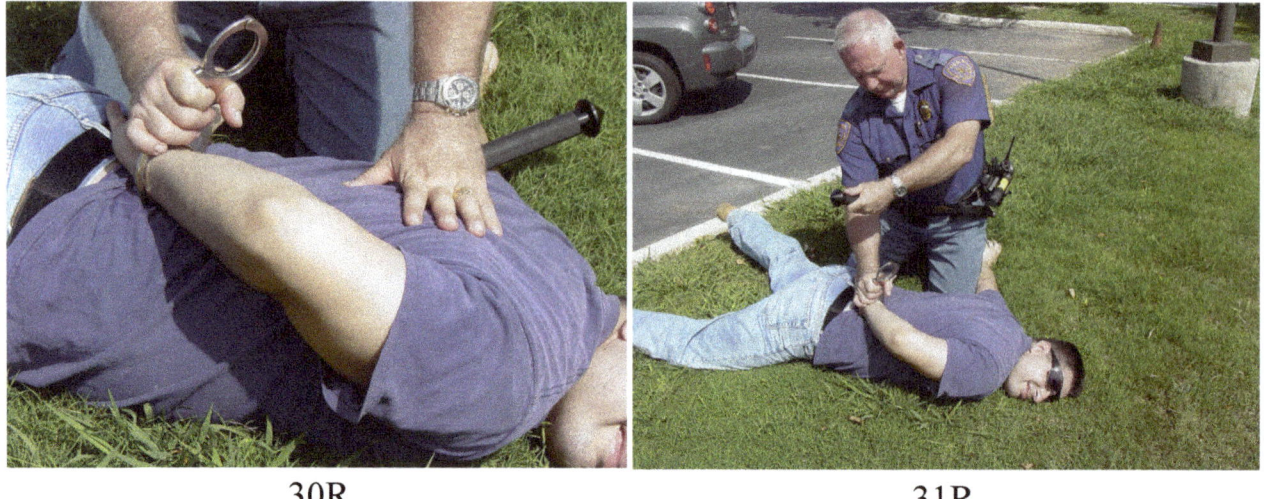

30R　　　　　　　　　　　　31R

Figure (30R) Once the cuff is secure, keep a good grip on the cuff with your right hand and shift you weight off the baton and remove the baton end from under his abdominal area.

Figure (31R) Now the baton is removed completely from any contact with the actor, but the knee is still behind his arm. The baton needs to be placed so it can not be picked up by the actor or someone close by. In this case, I am carrying a (RCB) Baton and I slide it back through the baton holder. With other batons, slide it back in the baton loop or where it is not available to be picked up.

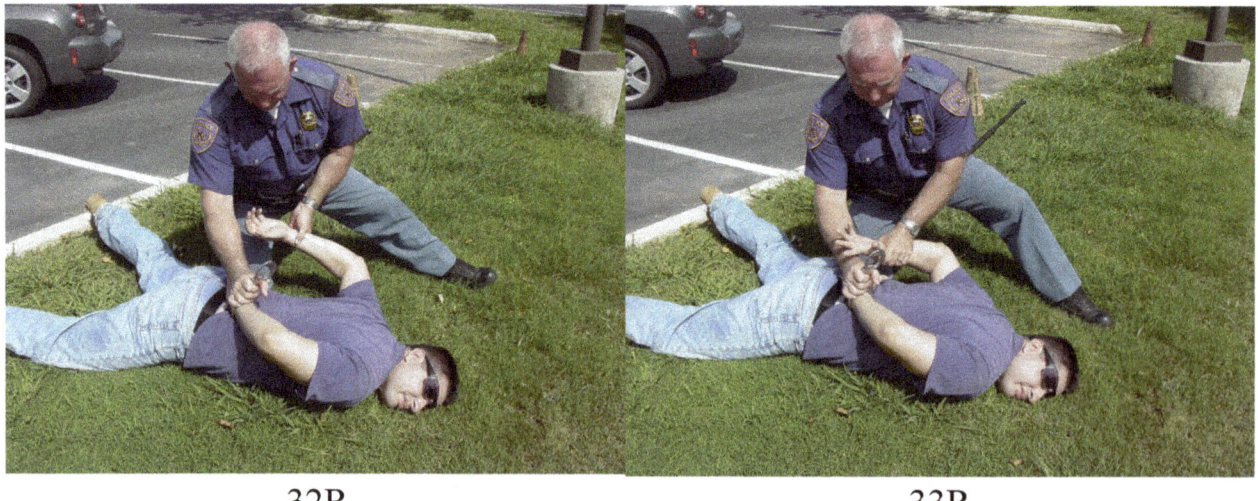

32R　　　　　　　　　　　　33R

Figure (32R) Extend your leg to allow the actor's arm to come back as you grab his wrist and bring it around. Keeping the cuffed hand in the small of his back.

Figure (33R) When bringing his hand around, bring it over and past the cuff and place it down on the cuff so the cuff will ratchet around the actor's wrist. ***(Again it is easier when using a Hinge or Ridged cuff so it will not turn.)***

STANDING YOUR PRISONER

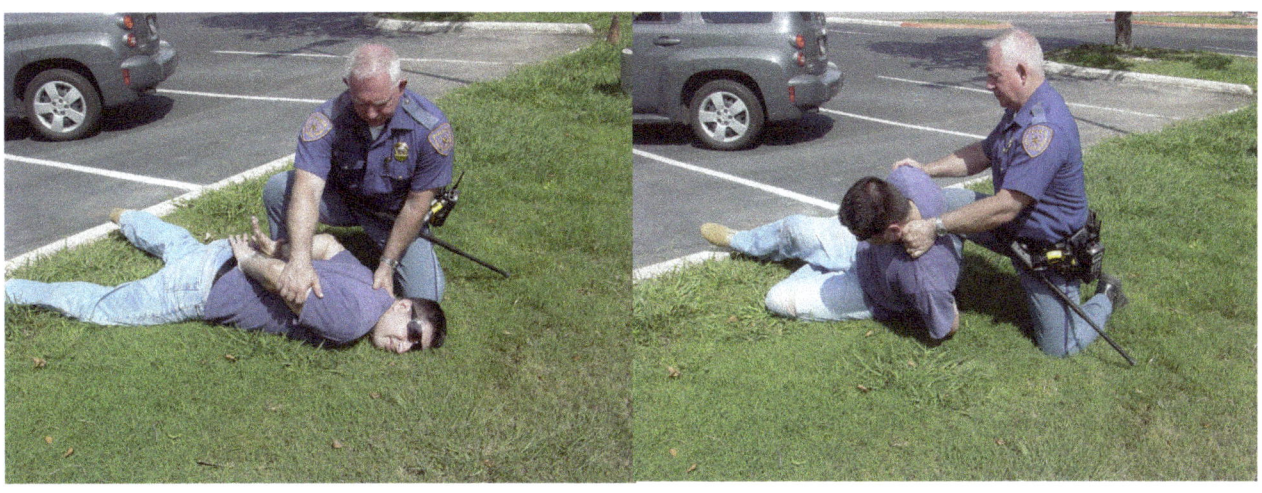

34R   35R

Figure (34Q) After cuffs are applied advise prisoner he is going to be sat up so he knows what your intentions are. Reach across, grabbing his far arm turning him back to you and facing away from you.

Figure (36Q) As you pull him up to a seated position, instruct him to bend his left knee.

36R   37R

Figure (36R) Sitting him up with his leg bent under the opposite leg and keeping his balance forward, bring your knee up to his back in case that he may try to push back on you. Keep you head up so your face is not close to the back of his head, in case he should throw his head back.

Figure (37R) Instruct your prisoner that you are going to stand him up by pushing forward onto his knee.

38R 39R

Figure (38R) Have your prisoner step forward with his right leg to become stable before standing.

Figure (39R) After he is stable, reach inside the handcuff gripping his ring and little finger, pulling them upward in the cuff for control.

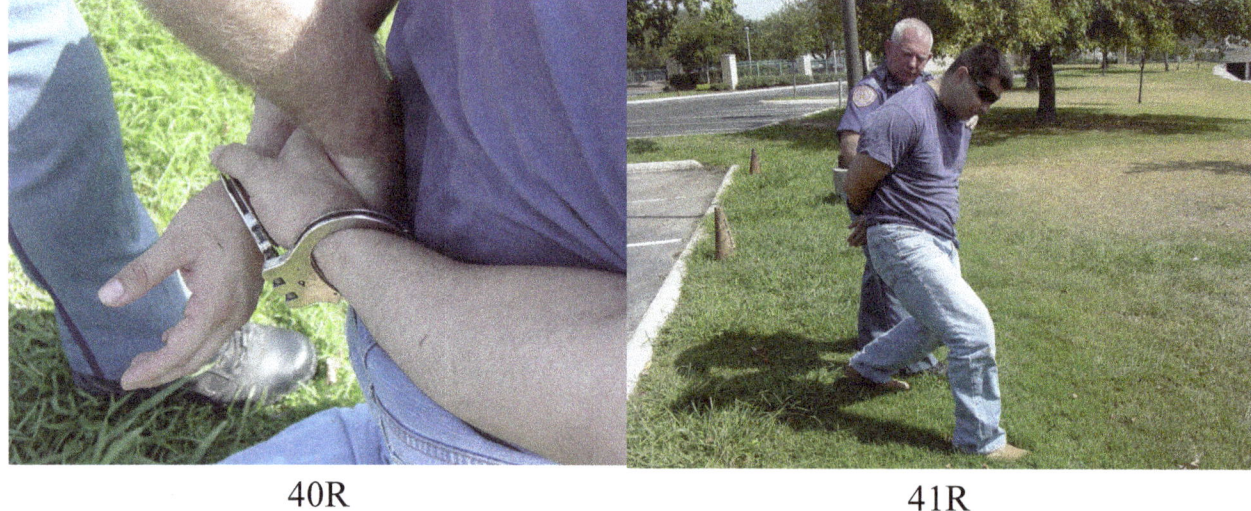

40R 41R

Figure (40R) In this picture, the hands are in opposite directions in the handcuffs. Grip the inside of his hand, little finger side, grasping the ring and little finger. Get this grip on his fingers when you stand him to his feet. He will not want to run when his fingers are in this position. This also works well when both hands are cuffed in the down position, and works best when handcuffed with Hinge or Ridged cuffs. If chain cuffs are used, the wrist will be able to rotate around and there is no point where the cuffs stop the up pulling on the fingers.

Figure (41R) Let your intentions be known to your prisoner. Give him specific orders to walk, stand, sit, or whatever is needed on your behalf.

42R

Figure (42R) A good grip on your prisoner's fingers means complete control and is painful. Only apply as much pressure as needed to move your prisoner. Remember that pain does breed control. In practice, be careful not to be over anxious to stand your partner. After this is applied a few times in practice, the fingers get a little sore. (*ALWAYS USE CAUTION ON YOUR PRACTICE PARTNER*)

IN CLOSING

I would like to give a special thanks to the many officers that have purchased this book and also to the officers that have taken time out of their busy schedules to take this course. I hope this book has given you a different perspective on the uses of the baton. My hopes are that you will be able to put the baton in your arsenal of weapons as more than a "knocking on doors" or a "striking" tool.

In today's world of video technology and civilian scrutiny of police officers, the use of your baton can be an asset to you if used in the manner of a great tactical instrument.

It has been a pleasure writing and doing these classes to assist my brother officers. It is my hope that this book can give you a little more tactical advantage than you had before. Please take care of your fellow officer and communities out there. Be alert, Be safe, and God Speed.

Sincere thanks,

Gary G. Albrecht

www.ingramcontent.com/pod-product-compliance
Lightning Source LLC
Chambersburg PA
CBHW060942170426
43196CB00024B/2965